Contents

Introduction

Part One VISION
1. Start
2. Define
3. Learn
4. Experiment

Part Two STEER
5. Leap
6. Test
7. Measure
8. Pivot (or Persevere)

Part Three ACCELERATE
9. Batch
10. Grow
11. Adapt
12. Innovate

13. Epilogue: Waste Not

Introduction

Stop me if you've heard this one before. Brilliant college kids sitting in a dorm are inventing the future. Heedless of boundaries, possessed of new technology and youthful enthusiasm, they build a new company from scratch. Their early success allows them to raise money and bring an amazing new product to market. They hire their friends, assemble a superstar team, and dare the world to stop them.

Ten years and several startups ago, that was me, building my first company. I particularly remember a moment from back then: the moment I realized my company was going to fail. My cofounder and I were at our wits' end. The dot-com bubble had burst, and we had spent all our money. We tried desperately to raise more capital, and we could not. It was like a breakup scene from a Hollywood movie: it was raining, and we were arguing in the street. We couldn't even agree on where to walk next, and so we parted in anger, heading in opposite directions. As a metaphor for our company's failure, this image of the two of us, lost in the rain and drifting apart, is perfect.

It remains a painful memory. The company limped along for months afterward, but our situation was hopeless. At the time, it had seemed we were doing everything right: we had a great product, a brilliant team, amazing technology, and the right idea at the right time. And we really were on to something. We were building a way for college kids to create online profiles for the purpose of sharing . . . with employers. Oops. But despite a promising idea, we were nonetheless doomed from day one, because we did not know the process we would need to use to turn our product insights into a great company.

If you've never experienced a failure like this, it is hard to describe the feeling. It's as if the world were falling out from under you. You realize you've been duped. The stories in the magazines are lies: hard work and perseverance don't lead to success. Even worse, the many, many, many promises you've made to employees, friends, and family are not going to come true. Everyone who thought you were foolish for stepping out on your own will be proven right.

It wasn't supposed to turn out that way. In magazines and newspapers, in blockbuster movies, and on countless blogs, we hear the mantra of the successful entrepreneurs: through determination, brilliance, great timing, and—above all—a great product, you too can achieve fame and fortune.

There is a mythmaking industry hard at work to sell us that story, but I have come to believe that the story is false, the product of selection bias and after-the-fact rationalization. In fact, having worked with hundreds of entrepreneurs, I have seen firsthand how often a promising start leads to failure. The grim reality is that most startups fail. Most new products are not successful. Most new ventures do not live up to their potential.

Yet the story of perseverance, creative genius, and hard work persists. Why is it so popular? I think there is something deeply appealing about this modern-day rags-to-riches story. It makes success seem inevitable if you just have the right stuff. It means that the mundane details, the boring stuff, the small individual choices don't matter. If we build it, they will come. When we fail, as so many of us do, we have a ready-made excuse: we didn't have the right stuff. We weren't visionary enough or weren't in the right place at the right time.

After more than ten years as an entrepreneur, I came to reject that line of thinking. I have learned from both my own successes and failures and those of many others that it's the boring stuff that matters the most. Startup success is not a consequence of good genes or being in the right place at the right time. Startup success can be engineered by following the right process, which means it can be learned, which means it can be taught.

Entrepreneurship is a kind of management. No, you didn't read that wrong. We have wildly divergent associations with these two words, *entrepreneurship* and *management*. Lately, it seems that one is cool, innovative, and exciting and the other is dull, serious, and bland. It is time to look past these preconceptions.

Let me tell you a second startup story. It's 2004, and a group of founders have just started a new company. Their previous company had failed very publicly. Their credibility is at an all-time low. They have a huge vision: to change the way people communicate by using a new technology called avatars (remember, this was before James Cameron's blockbuster movie). They are following a visionary named Will Harvey, who paints a compelling picture: people connecting with their friends, hanging out online, using avatars to give them a combination of intimate connection and safe anonymity. Even better, instead of having to build all the clothing, furniture, and accessories these avatars would need to accessorize their digital lives, the customers would be enlisted to build those things and sell them to one another.

The engineering challenge before them is immense: creating virtual worlds, user-generated content, an online commerce engine, micropayments, and—last but not least—the three-dimensional avatar technology that can run on anyone's PC.

I'm in this second story, too. I'm a cofounder and chief technology officer of this company, which is called IMVU. At this point in our careers, my cofounders and I are determined to make new mistakes. We do everything wrong: instead of spending years perfecting our technology, we build a minimum viable product, an early product that is terrible, full of bugs and crash-your-computer-yes-really stability problems. Then we ship it to customers way before it's ready. And we charge money for it. After securing initial customers, we change the product constantly—much too fast by traditional standards—shipping new versions of our product dozens of times every single day.

We really did have customers in those early days—true visionary early adopters—and we often talked to them and asked for their feedback. But we emphatically did *not* do what they said. We viewed their input as only one source of information about our product and overall vision. In fact, we were much more likely to run experiments on our customers than we were to cater to their whims.

Traditional business thinking says that this approach shouldn't work, but it does, and you don't have to take my word for it. As you'll see throughout this book, the approach we pioneered at IMVU has become the basis for a new movement of entrepreneurs around the world. It builds on many previous management and product development ideas, including lean manufacturing, design thinking, customer development, and agile development. It represents a new approach to creating continuous innovation. It's called the Lean Startup.

Despite the volumes written on business strategy, the key attributes of business leaders, and ways to identify the next big thing, innovators still struggle to bring their ideas to life. This was the frustration that led us to try a radical new approach at IMVU, one characterized by an extremely fast cycle time, a focus on what customers want (without asking them), and a scientific approach to making decisions.

ORIGINS OF THE LEAN STARTUP

I am one of those people who grew up programming computers, and so my journey to thinking about entrepreneurship and management has taken a circuitous path. I have always worked on the product development side of my industry; my partners and bosses were managers or marketers, and my peers worked in engineering and operations. Throughout my career, I kept having the experience of working incredibly hard on products that ultimately failed in the marketplace.

At first, largely because of my background, I viewed these as technical problems that required technical solutions: better architecture, a better engineering process, better discipline, focus, or product vision. These supposed fixes led to still more failure. So I read everything I could get my hands on and was blessed to have had some of the top minds in Silicon Valley as my mentors. By the time I became a cofounder of IMVU, I was hungry for new ideas about how to build a company.

I was fortunate to have cofounders who were willing to experiment with new approaches. They were fed up—as I was—by the failure of traditional thinking. Also, we were lucky to have Steve Blank as an investor and adviser. Back in 2004, Steve had just begun preaching a new idea: the business and marketing functions of a startup should be considered as important as engineering and product development and therefore deserve an equally rigorous methodology to guide them. He called that methodology Customer Development, and it offered insight and guidance to my daily work as an entrepreneur.

Meanwhile, I was building IMVU's product development team, using some of the unorthodox methods I mentioned earlier. Measured against the traditional theories of product development I had been trained on in my career, these methods did not make sense, yet I could see firsthand that they were working. I struggled to explain the practices to new employees, investors, and the founders of other companies. We lacked a common language for describing them and concrete principles for understanding them.

I began to search outside entrepreneurship for ideas that could help me make sense of my experience. I began to study other industries, especially manufacturing, from which most modern theories of management derive. I studied lean manufacturing, a process that originated in Japan with the Toyota Production System, a completely new way of thinking about the manufacturing of physical goods. I found that by applying ideas from lean manufacturing to my own entrepreneurial challenges—with a few tweaks and changes—I had the beginnings of a framework for making sense of them.

This line of thought evolved into the Lean Startup: the application of lean thinking to the process of innovation.

IMVU became a tremendous success. IMVU customers have created more than 60 million avatars. It is a profitable company with annual revenues of more than $50 million in 2011, employing more than a hundred people in our current offices in Mountain View, California. IMVU's virtual goods catalog—which seemed so risky years ago—now has more than 6 million items in it; more than 7,000 are added every day, almost all created by customers.

As a result of IMVU's success, I began to be asked for advice by other startups and venture capitalists. When I would describe my experiences at IMVU, I was often met with blank stares or extreme skepticism. The most common reply was "That could never work!" My experience so flew in the face of conventional thinking that most people, even in the innovation hub of Silicon Valley, could not wrap their minds around it.

Then I started to write, first on a blog called *Startup Lessons Learned,* and speak—at conferences and to companies, startups, and venture capitalists—to anyone who would listen. In the process of being called on to defend and explain my insights and with the collaboration of other writers, thinkers, and entrepreneurs, I had a chance to refine and develop the theory of the Lean Startup beyond its rudimentary beginnings. My hope all along was to find ways to eliminate the tremendous waste I saw all around me: startups that built products nobody wanted, new products pulled from the shelves, countless dreams unrealized.

Eventually, the Lean Startup idea blossomed into a global movement. Entrepreneurs began forming local in-person groups to discuss and apply Lean Startup ideas. There are now organized communities of practice in more than a hundred cities around the world.[1] My travels have taken me across countries and continents. Everywhere I have seen the signs of a new entrepreneurial renaissance. The Lean Startup movement is making entrepreneurship accessible to a whole new generation of founders who are hungry for new ideas about how to build successful companies.

Although my background is in high-tech software entrepreneurship, the movement has grown way beyond those roots. Thousands of entrepreneurs are putting Lean Startup principles to work in every conceivable industry. I've had the chance to work with entrepreneurs in companies of all sizes, in different industries, and even in government. This journey has taken me to places I never imagined I'd see, from the world's most elite venture capitalists, to Fortune 500 boardrooms, to the Pentagon. The most nervous I have ever been in a meeting was when

I was attempting to explain Lean Startup principles to the chief information officer of the U.S. Army, who is a three-star general (for the record, he was extremely open to new ideas, even from a civilian like me).

Pretty soon I realized that it was time to focus on the Lean Startup movement full time. My mission: to improve the success rate of new innovative products worldwide. The result is the book you are reading.

THE LEAN STARTUP METHOD

This is a book for entrepreneurs and the people who hold them accountable. The five principles of the Lean Startup, which inform all three parts of this book, are as follows:

1. Entrepreneurs are everywhere. You don't have to work in a garage to be in a startup. The concept of entrepreneurship includes anyone who works within my definition of a startup: a human institution designed to create new products and services under conditions of extreme uncertainty. That means entrepreneurs are everywhere and the Lean Startup approach can work in any size company, even a very large enterprise, in any sector or industry.

2. Entrepreneurship is management. A startup is an institution, not just a product, and so it requires a new kind of management specifically geared to its context of extreme uncertainty. In fact, as I will argue later, I believe "entrepreneur" should be considered a job title in all modern companies that depend on innovation for their future growth.

3. Validated learning. Startups exist not just to make stuff, make money, or even serve customers. They exist to *learn* how to build a sustainable business. This learning can be validated scientifically by running frequent experiments that allow entrepreneurs to test each element of their vision.

4. Build-Measure-Learn. The fundamental activity of a startup is to turn ideas into products, measure how customers respond, and then learn whether to pivot or persevere. All successful startup processes should be geared to accelerate that feedback loop.

5. Innovation accounting. To improve entrepreneurial outcomes and hold innovators accountable, we need to focus on the boring stuff: how to measure progress, how to set up milestones, and how to prioritize work. This requires a new kind of accounting designed for startups—and the people who hold them accountable.

Why Startups Fail

Why are startups failing so badly everywhere we look?

The first problem is the allure of a good plan, a solid strategy, and thorough market research. In earlier eras, these things were indicators of likely success. The overwhelming temptation is to apply them to startups too, but this doesn't work, because startups operate with too much uncertainty. Startups do not yet know who their customer is or what their product should be. As the world becomes more uncertain, it gets harder and harder to predict the future. The old management methods are not up to the task. Planning and forecasting are only accurate when based on a long, stable operating history and a relatively static environment. Startups have neither.

The second problem is that after seeing traditional management fail to solve this problem, some entrepreneurs and investors have thrown up their hands and adopted the "Just Do It" school of startups. This school believes that if management is the problem, chaos is the answer. Unfortunately, as I can attest firsthand, this doesn't work either.

It may seem counterintuitive to think that something as disruptive, innovative, and chaotic as a startup can be managed or, to be accurate, *must* be managed. Most people think of process and management as boring and dull, whereas startups are dynamic and exciting. But what is actually exciting is to see startups succeed and change the world. The passion, energy, and vision that people bring to these new ventures are resources too precious to waste. We can—and must—do better. This book is about how.

HOW THIS BOOK IS ORGANIZED

This book is divided into three parts: "Vision," "Steer," and "Accelerate."

"Vision" makes the case for a new discipline of entrepreneurial management. I identify who is an entrepreneur, define a startup, and articulate a new way for startups to gauge if they are making progress, called validated learning. To achieve that learning, we'll see that startups—in a garage or inside an enterprise—can use scientific experimentation to discover how to build a sustainable business.

"Steer" dives into the Lean Startup method in detail, showing one major turn through the core Build-Measure-Learn feedback loop. Beginning with leap-of-faith assumptions that cry out for rigorous testing, you'll learn how to build a minimum viable product to test those assumptions, a new accounting system for evaluating whether you're making progress, and a method for deciding whether to pivot (changing course with one foot anchored to the ground) or persevere.

In "Accelerate," we'll explore techniques that enable Lean Startups to speed through the Build-Measure-Learn feedback loop as quickly as possible, even as they scale. We'll explore lean manufacturing concepts that are applicable to startups, too, such as the power of small batches. We'll also discuss organizational design, how products grow, and how to apply Lean Startup principles beyond the proverbial garage, even inside the world's largest companies.

MANAGEMENT'S SECOND CENTURY

As a society, we have a proven set of techniques for managing big companies and we know the best practices for building physical products. But when it comes to startups and innovation, we are still shooting in the dark. We are relying on vision, chasing the "great men" who can make magic happen, or trying to analyze our new products to death. These are new problems, born of the success of management in the twentieth century.

This book attempts to put entrepreneurship and innovation on a rigorous footing. We are at the dawn of management's second century. It is our challenge to do something great with the opportunity we have been given. The Lean Startup movement seeks to ensure that those of us who long to build the next big thing will have the tools we need to change the world.

Continue Book 1

7
MEASURE

At the beginning, a startup is little more than a model on a piece of paper. The financials in the business plan include projections of how many customers the company expects to attract, how much it will spend, and how much revenue and profit that will lead to. It's an ideal that's usually far from where the startup is in its early days.

A startup's job is to (1) rigorously measure where it is right now, confronting the hard truths that assessment reveals, and then (2) devise experiments to learn how to move the real numbers closer to the ideal reflected in the business plan.

Most products—even the ones that fail—do not have zero traction. Most products have some customers, some growth, and some positive results. One of the most dangerous outcomes for a startup is to bumble along in the land of the living dead. Employees and entrepreneurs tend to be optimistic by nature. We want to keep believing in our ideas even when the writing is on the wall. This is why the myth of perseverance is so dangerous. We all know stories of epic entrepreneurs who managed to pull out a victory when things seemed incredibly bleak. Unfortunately, we don't hear stories about the countless nameless others who persevered too long, leading their companies to failure.

WHY SOMETHING AS SEEMINGLY DULL AS ACCOUNTING WILL CHANGE YOUR LIFE

People are accustomed to thinking of accounting as dry and boring, a necessary evil used primarily to prepare financial reports and survive audits, but that is because accounting is something that has become taken for granted. Historically, under the leadership of people such as Alfred Sloan at General Motors, accounting became an essential part of the method of exerting centralized control over far-flung divisions. Accounting allowed GM to set clear milestones for each of its divisions and then hold each manager accountable for his or her division's success in reaching those goals. All modern corporations use some variation of that approach. Accounting is the key to their success.

Unfortunately, standard accounting is not helpful in evaluating entrepreneurs. Startups are too unpredictable for forecasts and milestones to be accurate.

I recently met with a phenomenal startup team. They are well financed, have significant customer traction, and are growing rapidly. Their product is a leader in an emerging category of enterprise software that uses consumer marketing techniques to sell into large companies. For example, they rely on employee-to-employee viral adoption rather than a traditional sales process, which might target the chief information officer or the head of information technology (IT). As a result, they have the opportunity to use cutting-edge experimental techniques as they constantly revise their product. During the meeting, I asked the team a simple question that I make a habit of asking startups whenever we meet: are you making your product better? They always say yes. Then I ask: how do you know? I invariably get this answer: well, we are in engineering and we made a number of changes last month, and our customers seem to like them, and our overall numbers are higher this month. We must be on the right track.

This is the kind of storytelling that takes place at most startup board meetings. Most milestones are built the same way: hit a certain product milestone, maybe talk to a few customers, and see if the numbers go up. Unfortunately, this is not a good indicator of whether a startup is making progress. How do we know that the changes we've made are related to the results we're seeing? More important, how do we know that we are drawing the right lessons from those changes?

To answer these kinds of questions, startups have a strong need for a new kind of accounting geared specifically to disruptive innovation. That's what innovation accounting is.

An Accountability Framework That Works Across Industries

Innovation accounting enables startups to prove objectively that they are learning how to grow a sustainable business. Innovation accounting begins by turning the leap-of-faith assumptions discussed in Chapter 5 into a quantitative financial model. Every business plan has some kind of model associated with it, even if it's written on the back of a napkin. That model provides assumptions about what the business will look like at a successful point in the future.

For example, the business plan for an established manufacturing company would show it growing in proportion to its sales volume. As the profits from the sales of goods are reinvested in marketing and promotions, the company gains new customers. The rate of growth depends primarily on three things: the profitability of each customer, the cost of acquiring new customers, and the repeat purchase rate of existing customers. The higher these values are, the faster the company will grow and the more profitable it will be. These are the drivers of the company's growth model.

By contrast, a marketplace company that matches buyers and sellers such as eBay will have a different growth model. Its success depends primarily on the network effects that make it the premier destination for both buyers and sellers to transact business. Sellers want the marketplace with the highest number of potential customers. Buyers want the marketplace with the most competition among sellers, which leads to the greatest availability of products and the lowest prices. (In economics, this sometimes is called supply-side increasing returns and demand-side increasing returns.) For this kind of startup, the important thing to measure is that the network effects are working, as evidenced by the high retention rate of new buyers and sellers. If people stick with the product with very little attrition, the marketplace will grow no matter how the company acquires new customers. The growth curve will look like a compounding interest table, with the rate of growth depending on the "interest rate" of new customers coming to the product.

Though these two businesses have very different drivers of growth, we can still use a common framework to hold their leaders accountable. This framework supports accountability even when the model changes.

HOW INNOVATION ACCOUNTING WORKS—THREE LEARNING MILESTONES

Innovation accounting works in three steps: first, use a minimum viable product to establish real data on where the company is right now. Without a clear-eyed picture of your current status—no matter how far from the goal you may be—you cannot begin to track your progress.

Second, startups must attempt to tune the engine from the baseline toward the ideal. This may take many attempts. After the startup has made all the micro changes and product optimizations it can to move its baseline toward the ideal, the company reaches a decision point. That is the third step: pivot or persevere.

If the company is making good progress toward the ideal, that means it's learning appropriately and using that learning effectively, in which case it makes sense to continue. If not, the management team eventually must conclude that its current product strategy is flawed and needs a serious change. When a company pivots, it starts the process all over again, reestablishing a new baseline and then tuning the engine from there. The sign of a successful pivot is that these engine-tuning activities are more productive after the pivot than before.

Establish the Baseline

For example, a startup might create a complete prototype of its product and offer to sell it to real customers through its main marketing channel. This single MVP would test most of the startup's assumptions and establish baseline metrics for each assumption simultaneously. Alternatively, a startup might prefer to build separate MVPs that are aimed at getting feedback on one assumption at a time. Before building the prototype, the company might perform a smoke test with its marketing materials. This is an old direct marketing technique in which customers are given the opportunity to preorder a product that has not yet been built. A smoke test measures only one thing: whether customers are interested in trying a product. By itself, this is insufficient to validate an entire growth model. Nonetheless, it can be very useful to get feedback on this assumption before committing more money and other resources to the product.

These MVPs provide the first example of a *learning milestone*. An MVP allows a startup to fill in real baseline data in its growth model—conversion rates, sign-up and trial rates, customer lifetime value, and so on—and this is valuable as the foundation for learning about customers and their reactions to a product even if that foundation begins with extremely bad news.

When one is choosing among the many assumptions in a business plan, it makes sense to test the riskiest assumptions first. If you can't find a way to mitigate these risks toward the ideal that is required for a sustainable business, there is no point in testing the others. For example, a media business that is selling advertising has two basic assumptions that take the form of questions: Can it capture the attention of a defined customer segment on an ongoing basis? and can it sell that attention to advertisers? In a business in which the advertising rates for a particular customer segment are well known, the far riskier assumption is the ability to capture attention. Therefore, the first experiments should involve content production rather than advertising sales. Perhaps the company will produce a pilot episode or issue to see how customers engage.

Tuning the Engine

Once the baseline has been established, the startup can work toward the second learning milestone: tuning the engine. Every product development, marketing, or other initiative that a startup undertakes should be targeted at improving one of the drivers of its growth model. For example, a company might spend time improving the design of its product to make it easier for new customers to use. This presupposes that the *activation rate* of new customers is a driver of growth and that its baseline is lower than the company would like. To demonstrate validated learning, the design changes must improve the activation rate of new customers. If they do not, the new design should be judged a failure. This is an important rule: a good design is one that changes customer behavior for the better.

Compare two startups. The first company sets out with a clear baseline metric, a hypothesis about what will improve that metric, and a set of experiments designed to test that hypothesis. The second team sits around debating what would improve the product, implements several of those changes at once, and celebrates if there is any positive increase in any of the numbers. Which startup is more likely to be doing effective work and achieving lasting results?

Pivot or Persevere

Over time, a team that is learning its way toward a sustainable business will see the numbers in its model rise from the horrible baseline established by the MVP and converge to something like the ideal one established in the business plan. A startup that fails to do so will see that ideal recede ever farther into the distance. When this is done right, even the most powerful reality distortion field won't be able to cover up this simple fact: if we're not moving the drivers of our business model, we're not making progress. That becomes a sure sign that it's time to pivot.

INNOVATION ACCOUNTING AT IMVU

Here's what innovation accounting looked like for us in the early days of IMVU. Our minimum viable product had many defects and, when we first released it, extremely low sales. We naturally assumed that the lack of sales was related to the low quality of the product, so week after week we worked on improving the quality of the product, trusting that our efforts were worthwhile. At the end of each month, we would have a board meeting at which we would present the results. The night before the board meeting, we'd run our standard analytics, measuring conversion rates, customer counts, and revenue to show what a good job we had done. For several meetings in a row, this caused a last-minute panic because the quality improvements were not yielding any change in customer behavior. This led to some frustrating board meetings at which we could show great product "progress" but not much in the way of business results. After a while, rather than leave it to the last minute, we began to track our metrics more frequently, tightening the feedback loop with product development. This was even more depressing. Week in, week out, our product changes were having no effect.

Improving a Product on Five Dollars a Day

We tracked the "funnel metrics" behaviors that were critical to our engine of growth: customer registration, the download of our application, trial, repeat usage, and purchase. To have enough data to learn, we needed just enough customers using our product to get real numbers for each behavior. We allocated a budget of five dollars per day: enough to buy clicks on the then-new Google AdWords system. In those days, the minimum you could bid for a click was 5 cents, but there was no overall minimum to your spending. Thus, we could afford to open an account and get started even though we had very little money.[1]

Five dollars bought us a hundred clicks—every day. From a marketing point of view this was not very significant, but for learning it was priceless. Every single day we were able to measure our product's performance with a brand new set of customers. Also, each time we revised the product, we got a brand new report card on how we were doing the very next day.

For example, one day we would debut a new marketing

message aimed at first-time customers. The next day we might change the way new customers were initiated into the product. Other days, we would add new features, fix bugs, roll out a new visual design, or try a new layout for our website. Every time, we told ourselves we were making the product better, but that subjective confidence was put to the acid test of real numbers.

Day in and day out we were performing random trials. Each day was a new experiment. Each day's customers were independent of those of the day before. Most important, even though our gross numbers were growing, it became clear that our funnel metrics were not changing.

Here is a graph from one of IMVU's early board meetings:

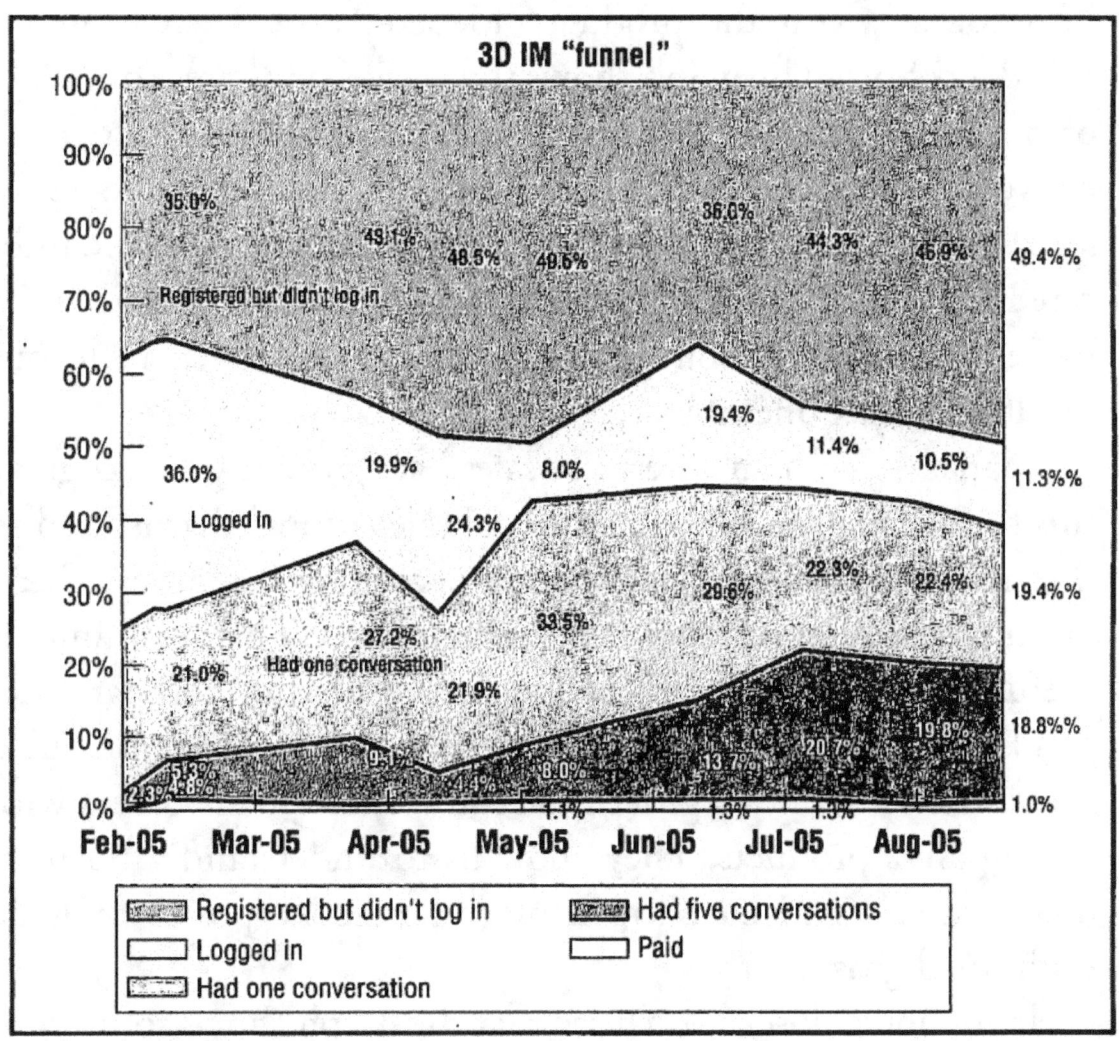

This graph represents approximately seven months of work. Over that period, we were making constant improvements to the IMVU product, releasing new features on a daily basis. We were conducting a lot of in-person customer interviews, and our product development team was working extremely hard.

Cohort Analysis

To read the graph, you need to understand something called *cohort analysis.* This is one of the most important tools of startup analytics. Although it sounds complex, it is based on a simple premise. Instead of looking at cumulative totals or gross numbers such as total revenue and total number of customers, one looks at the performance of each group of customers that comes into contact with the product independently. Each group is called a cohort. The graph shows the conversion rates to IMVU of new customers who joined in each indicated month. Each conversion rate shows the percentage of customer who registered in that month who subsequently went on to take the indicated action. Thus, among all the customers who joined IMVU in February 2005, about 60 percent of them logged in to our product at least one time.

Managers with an enterprise sales background will recognize this funnel analysis as the traditional sales funnel that is used to manage prospects on their way to becoming customers. Lean Startups use it in product development, too. This technique is useful in many types of business, because every company depends for its survival on sequences of customer behavior called flows. Customer flows govern the interaction of customers with a company's products. They allow us to understand a business quantitatively and have much more predictive power than do traditional gross metrics.

If you look closely, you'll see that the graph shows some clear trends. Some product improvements are helping—a little. The percentage of new customers who go on to use the product at least five times has grown from less than 5 percent to almost 20 percent. Yet despite this fourfold increase, the percentage of new customers who pay money for IMVU is stuck at around 1 percent. Think about that for a moment. After months and months of work, thousands of individual improvements, focus groups, design sessions, and usability tests, the percentage of new customers who subsequently pay money is exactly the same as it was at the onset even though many more customers are getting a chance to try the product.

Thanks to the power of cohort analysis, we could not blame this failure on the legacy of previous customers who were resistant to change, external market conditions, or any other excuse. Each cohort represented an independent report card, and try as we might, we were getting straight C's. This helped us realize we had a problem.

I was in charge of the product development team, small though it was in those days, and shared with my cofounders the sense that the problem had to be with my team's efforts. I worked harder, tried to focus on higher- and higher-quality features, and lost a lot of sleep. Our frustration grew. When I could think of nothing else to do, I was finally ready to turn to the last resort: talking to customers. Armed with our failure to make progress tuning our engine of growth, I was ready to ask the right questions.

Before this failure, in the company's earliest days, it was easy to talk to potential customers and come away convinced we were on the right track. In fact, when we would invite customers into the office for in-person interviews and usability tests, it was easy to dismiss negative feedback. If they didn't want to use the product, I assumed they were not in our target market. "Fire that customer," I'd say to the person responsible for recruiting for our tests. "Find me someone in our target demographic." If the next customer was more positive, I would take it as confirmation that I was right in my targeting. If not, I'd fire another customer and try again.

By contrast, once I had data in hand, my interactions with customers changed. Suddenly I had urgent questions that needed answering: Why aren't customers responding to our product "improvements"? Why isn't our hard work paying off? For example, we kept making it easier and easier for customers to use IMVU with their existing friends. Unfortunately, customers didn't want to engage in that behavior. Making it easier to use was totally beside the point. Once we knew what to look for, genuine understanding came much faster. As was described in Chapter 3, this eventually led to a critically important pivot: away from an IM add-on used with existing friends and toward a stand-alone network one can use to make new friends. Suddenly, our worries about productivity vanished. Once our efforts were aligned with what customers really wanted, our experiments were much more likely to change their behavior for the better.

This pattern would repeat time and again, from the days when we were making less than a thousand dollars in revenue per month all the way up to the time we were making millions. In fact, this is the sign of a successful pivot: the new experiments you run are overall more productive than the experiments you were running before.

This is the pattern: poor quantitative results force us to declare failure and create the motivation, context, and space for more qualitative research. These investigations produce new ideas—new hypotheses—to be tested, leading to a possible pivot. Each pivot unlocks new opportunities for further experimentation, and the cycle repeats. Each time we repeat this simple rhythm: establish the baseline, tune the engine, and make a decision to pivot or persevere.

OPTIMIZATION VERSUS LEARNING

Engineers, designers, and marketers are all skilled at optimization. For example, direct marketers are experienced at split testing value propositions by sending a different offer to two similar groups of customers so that they can measure differences in the response rates of the two groups. Engineers, of course, are skilled at improving a product's performance, just as designers are talented at making products easier to use. All these activities in a well-run traditional organization offer incremental benefit for incremental effort. As long as we are executing the plan well, hard work yields results.

However, these tools for product improvement do not work the same way for startups. If you are building the wrong thing, optimizing the product or its marketing will not yield significant results. A startup has to measure progress against a high bar: evidence that a sustainable business can be built around its products or services. That's a standard that can be assessed only if a startup has made clear, tangible predictions ahead of time.

In the absence of those predictions, product and strategy decisions are far more difficult and time-consuming. I often see this in my consulting practice. I've been called in many times to help a startup that feels that its engineering team "isn't working hard enough." When I meet with those teams, there are always improvements to be made and I recommend them, but invariably the real problem is not a lack of development talent, energy, or effort. Cycle after cycle, the team is working hard, but the business is not seeing results. Managers trained in a traditional model draw the logical conclusion: our team is not working hard, not working effectively, or not working efficiently.

Thus the downward cycle begins: the product development team valiantly tries to build a product according to the specifications it is receiving from the creative or business leadership. When good results are not forthcoming, business leaders assume that any discrepancy between what was planned and what was built is the cause and try to specify the next iteration in greater detail. As the specifications get more detailed, the planning process slows down, batch size increases, and feedback is delayed. If a board of directors or CFO is involved as a stakeholder, it doesn't take long for personnel changes to follow.

A few years ago, a team that sells products to large media companies invited me to help them as a consultant because they were concerned that their engineers were not working hard enough. However, the fault was not in the engineers; it was in the process the whole company was using to make decisions. They had customers but did not know them very well. They were deluged with feature requests from customers, the internal sales team, and the business leadership. Every new insight became an emergency that had to be addressed immediately. As a result, long-term projects were hampered by constant interruptions. Even worse, the team had no clear sense of whether any of the changes they were making mattered to customers. Despite the constant tuning and tweaking, the business results were consistently mediocre.

Learning milestones prevent this negative spiral by emphasizing a more likely possibility: the company is executing—with discipline!—a plan that does not make sense. The innovation accounting framework makes it clear when the company is stuck and needs to change direction.

In the example above, early in the company's life, the product development team was incredibly productive because the company's founders had identified a large unmet need in the target market. The initial product, while flawed, was popular with early adopters. Adding the major features that customers asked for seemed to work wonders, as the early adopters spread the word about the innovation far and wide. But unasked and unanswered were other lurking questions: Did the company have a working engine of growth? Was this early success related to the daily work of the product development team? In most cases, the answer was no; success was driven by decisions the team had made in the past. None of its current initiatives were having any impact. But this was obscured because the company's gross metrics were all "up and to the right."

As we'll see in a moment, this is a common danger. Companies of any size that have a working engine of growth can come to rely on the wrong kind of metrics to guide their actions. This is what tempts managers to resort to the usual bag of success theater tricks: last-minute ad buys, channel stuffing, and whiz-bang demos, in a desperate attempt to make the gross numbers look better. Energy invested in success theater is energy that could have been used to help build a sustainable business. I call the traditional numbers used to judge startups "vanity metrics," and innovation accounting requires us to avoid the temptation to use them.

VANITY METRICS: A WORD OF CAUTION

To see the danger of vanity metrics clearly, let's return once more to the early days of IMVU. Take a look at the following graph, which is from the same era in IMVU's history as that shown earlier in this chapter. It covers the same time period as the cohort-style graph on page 122; in fact, it is from the same board presentation.

This graph shows the traditional gross metrics for IMVU so far: total registered users and total paying customers (the gross revenue graph looks almost the same). From this viewpoint, things look much more exciting. That's why I call these vanity

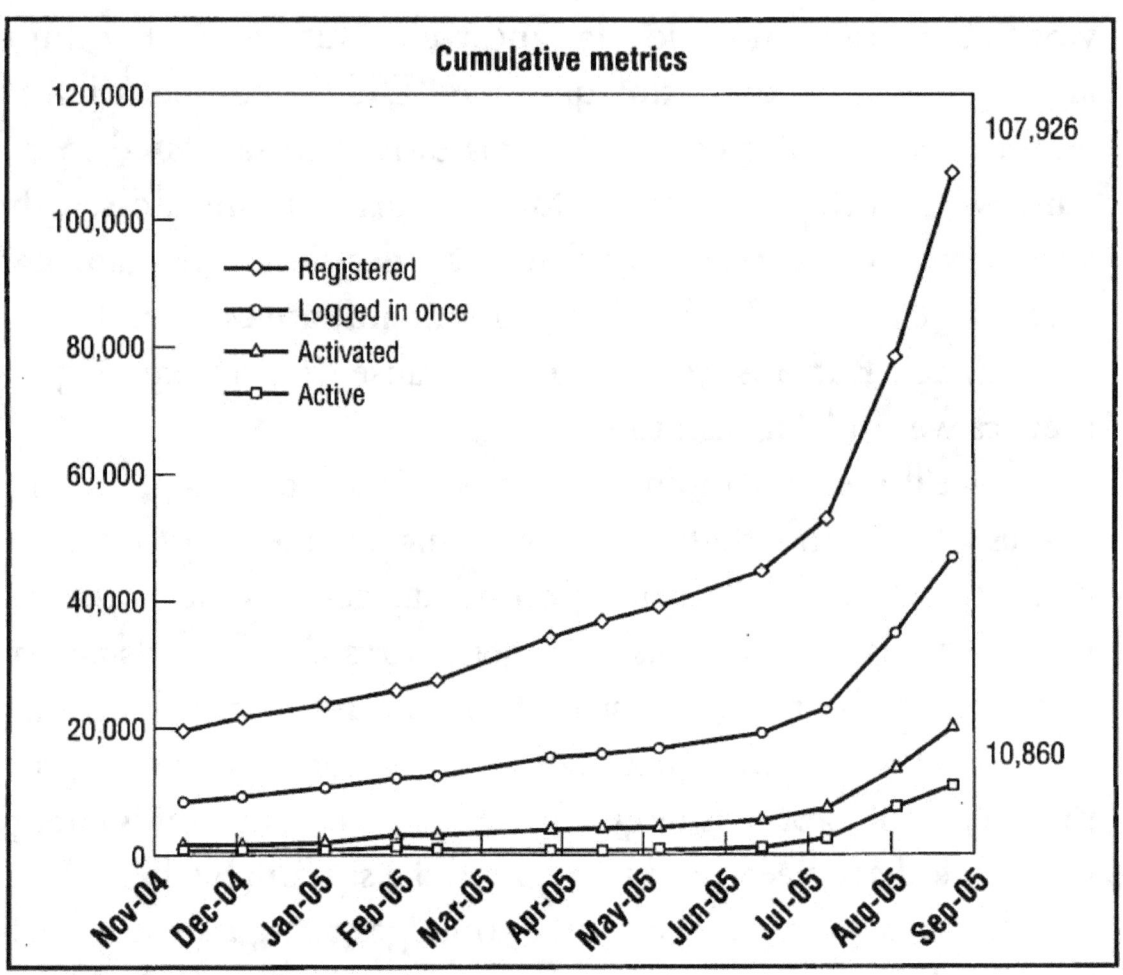

metrics: they give the rosiest possible picture. You'll see a traditional hockey stick graph (the ideal in a rapid-growth company). As long as you focus on the top-line numbers (signing up more customers, an increase in overall revenue), you'll be forgiven for thinking this product development team is making great progress. The company's growth engine is working. Each month it is able to acquire customers and has a positive return on investment. The excess revenue from those customers is reinvested the next month in acquiring more. That's where the growth is coming from.

But think back to the same data presented in a cohort style. IMVU is adding new customers, but it is not improving the yield on each new group. The engine is turning, but the efforts to tune the engine are not bearing much fruit. From the traditional graph alone, you cannot tell whether IMVU is on pace to build a sustainable business; you certainly can't tell anything about the efficacy of the entrepreneurial team behind it.

Innovation accounting will not work if a startup is being misled by these kinds of vanity metrics: gross number of customers and so on. The alternative is the kind of metrics we use to judge our business and our learning milestones, what I call *actionable metrics*.

ACTIONABLE METRICS VERSUS VANITY METRICS

To get a better sense of the importance of good metrics, let's look at a company called Grockit. Its founder, Farbood Nivi, spent a decade working as a teacher at two large for-profit education companies, Princeton Review and Kaplan, helping students prepare for standardized tests such as the GMAT, LSAT, and SAT. His engaging classroom style won accolades from his students and promotions from his superiors; he was honored with Princeton Review's National Teacher of the Year award. But Farb was frustrated with the traditional teaching methods used by those companies. Teaching six to nine hours per day to thousands of students, he had many opportunities to experiment with new approaches.[2]

Over time, Farb concluded that the traditional lecture model of education, with its one-to-many instructional approach, was inadequate for his students. He set out to develop a superior approach, using a combination of teacher-led lectures, individual homework, and group study. In particular, Farb was fascinated by how effective the student-to-student peer-driven learning method was for his students. When students could help each other, they benefited in two ways. First, they could get customized instruction from a peer who was much less intimidating than a teacher. Second, they could reinforce their learning by teaching it to others. Over time, Farb's classes became increasingly social—and successful.

As this unfolded, Farb felt more and more that his physical presence in the classroom was less important. He made an important connection: "I have this social learning model in my classroom. There's all this social stuff going on on the web." His idea was to bring social peer-to-peer learning to people who could not afford an expensive class from Kaplan or Princeton Review or an even more expensive private tutor. From this insight Grockit was born.

Farb explains, "Whether you're studying for the SAT or you're studying for algebra, you study in one of three ways. You spend some time with experts, you spend some time on your own, and you spend some time with your peers. Grockit offers these three same formats of studying. What we do is we apply technology and algorithms to optimize those three forms."

Farb is the classic entrepreneurial visionary. He recounts his original insight this way: "Let's forget educational design up until now, let's forget what's possible and just redesign learning with today's students and today's technology in mind. There were plenty of multi-billion-dollar organizations in the education space, and I don't think they were innovating in the way that we needed them to and I didn't think we needed them anymore. To me, it's really all about the students and I didn't feel like the students were being served as well as they could."

Today Grockit offers many different educational products, but in the beginning Farb followed a lean approach. Grockit built a minimum viable product, which was simply Farb teaching test prep via the popular online web conferencing tool WebEx. He built no custom software, no new technology. He simply attempted to bring his new teaching approach to students via the Internet. News about a new kind of private tutoring spread quickly, and within a few months Farb was making a decent living teaching online, with monthly revenues of $10,000 to $15,000. But like many entrepreneurs with ambition, Farb didn't build his MVP just to make a living. He had a vision of a more collaborative, more effective kind of teaching for students everywhere. With his initial traction, he was able to raise money from some of the most prestigious investors in Silicon Valley.

When I first met Farb, his company was already on the fast track to success. They had raised venture capital from well-regarded investors, had built an awesome team, and were fresh off an impressive debut at one of Silicon Valley's famous startup competitions.

They were extremely process-oriented and disciplined. Their product development followed a rigorous version of the agile development methodology known as Extreme Programming (described below), thanks to their partnership with a San Francisco–based company called Pivotal Labs. Their early product was hailed by the press as a breakthrough.

There was only one problem: they were not seeing sufficient growth in the use of the product by customers. Grockit is an excellent case study because its problems were not a matter of failure of execution or discipline.

Following standard agile practice, Grockit's work proceeded in a series of *sprints,* or one-month iteration cycles. For each sprint, Farb would prioritize the work to be done that month by writing a series of *user stories*, a technique taken from agile development. Instead of writing a specification for a new feature that described it in technical terms, Farb would write a story that described the feature from the point of view of the customer. That story helped keep the engineers focused on the customer's perspective throughout the development process.

Each feature was expressed in plain language in terms everyone could understand whether they had a technical background or not. Again following standard agile practice, Farb was free to reprioritize these stories at any time. As he learned more about what customers wanted, he could move things around in the *product backlog,* the queue of stories yet to be built. The only limit on this ability to change directions was that he could not interrupt any task that was in progress. Fortunately, the stories were written in such a way that the batch size of work (which I'll discuss in more detail in Chapter 9) was only a day or two.

This system is called agile development for a good reason: teams that employ it are able to change direction quickly, stay light on their feet, and be highly responsive to changes in the business requirements of the product owner (the manager of the process—in this case Farb—who is responsible for prioritizing the stories).

How did the team feel at the end of each sprint? They consistently delivered new product features. They would collect feedback from customers in the form of anecdotes and interviews that indicated that at least some customers liked the new features. There was always a certain amount of data that showed improvement: perhaps the total number of customers was increasing, the total number of questions answered by students was going up, or the number of returning customers was increasing.

However, I sensed that Farb and his team were left with lingering doubts about the company's overall progress. Was the increase in their numbers actually caused by their development efforts? Or could it be due to other factors, such as mentions of Grockit in the press? When I met the team, I asked them this simple question: How do you know that the prioritization decisions that Farb is making actually make sense?

Their answer: "That's not our department. Farb makes the decisions; we execute them."

At that time Grockit was focused on just one customer segment: prospective business school students who were studying for the GMAT. The product allowed students to engage in online study sessions with fellow students who were studying for the same exam. The product was working: the students who completed their studying via Grockit achieved significantly higher scores than they had before. But the Grockit team was struggling with the age-old startup problems: How do we know which features to prioritize? How can we get more customers to sign up and pay? How can we get out the word about our product?

I put this question to Farb: "How confident are you that you are making the right decisions in terms of establishing priorities?" Like most startup founders, he was looking at the available data and making the best educated guesses he could. But this left a lot of room for ambiguity and doubt.

Farb believed in his vision thoroughly and completely, yet he was starting to question whether his company was on pace to realize that vision. The product improved every day, but Farb wanted to make sure those improvements mattered to customers. I believe he deserves a lot of credit for realizing this. Unlike many visionaries, who cling to their original vision no matter what, Farb was willing to put his vision to the test.

Farb worked hard to sustain his team's belief that Grockit was destined for success. He was worried that morale would suffer if anyone thought that the person steering the ship was uncertain about which direction to go. Farb himself wasn't sure if his team would embrace a true learning culture. After all, this was part of the grand bargain of agile development: engineers agree to adapt the product to the business's constantly changing requirements but are not responsible for the quality of those business decisions.

Agile is an efficient system of development from the point of view of the developers. It allows them to stay focused on creating features and technical designs. An attempt to introduce the need to learn into that process could undermine productivity.

(Lean manufacturing faced similar problems when it was introduced in factories. Managers were used to focusing on the utilization rate of each machine. Factories were designed to keep machines running at full capacity as much of the time as possible. Viewed from the perspective of the machine, that is efficient, but from the point of view of the productivity of the entire factory, it is wildly inefficient at times. As they say in systems theory, that which optimizes one part of the system necessarily undermines the system as a whole.)

What Farb and his team didn't realize was that Grockit's progress was being measured by vanity metrics: the total number of customers and the total number of questions answered. That was what was causing his team to spin its wheels; those metrics gave the team the sensation of forward motion even though the company was making little progress. What's interesting is how closely Farb's method followed superficial aspects of the Lean Startup learning milestones: they shipped an early product and established some baseline metrics. They had relatively short iterations, each of which was judged by its ability to improve customer metrics.

However, because Grockit was using the wrong kinds of metrics, the startup was not genuinely improving. Farb was frustrated in his efforts to learn from customer feedback. In every cycle, the type of metrics his team was focused on would change: one month they would look at gross usage numbers, another month registration numbers, and so on. Those metrics would go up and down seemingly on their own. He couldn't draw clear cause-and-effect inferences. Prioritizing work correctly in such an environment is extremely challenging.

Farb could have asked his data analyst to investigate a

particular question. For example, when we shipped feature X, did it affect customer behavior? But that would have required tremendous time and effort. When, exactly, did feature X ship? Which customers were exposed to it? Was anything else launched around that same time? Were there seasonal factors that might be skewing the data? Finding these answers would have required parsing reams and reams of data. The answer often would come weeks after the question had been asked. In the meantime, the team would have moved on to new priorities and new questions that needed urgent attention.

Compared to a lot of startups, the Grockit team had a huge advantage: they were tremendously disciplined. A disciplined team may apply the wrong methodology but can shift gears quickly once it discovers its error. Most important, a disciplined team can experiment with its own working style and draw meaningful conclusions.

Cohorts and Split-tests

Grockit changed the metrics they used to evaluate success in two ways. Instead of looking at gross metrics, Grockit switched to cohort-based metrics, and instead of looking for cause-and-effect relationships after the fact, Grockit would launch each new feature as a true split-test experiment.

A split-test experiment is one in which different versions of a product are offered to customers at the same time. By observing the changes in behavior between the two groups, one can make inferences about the impact of the different variations. This technique was pioneered by direct mail advertisers. For example, consider a company that sends customers a catalog of products to buy, such as Lands' End or Crate & Barrel. If you wanted to test a catalog design, you could send a new version of it to 50 percent of the customers and send the old standard catalog to the other 50 percent. To assure a scientific result, both catalogs would contain identical products; the only difference would be the changes to the design. To figure out if the new design was effective, all you would have to do was keep track of the sales figures for both groups of customers. (This technique is sometimes called A/B testing after the practice of assigning letter names to each variation.) Although split testing often is thought of as a marketing-specific (or even a direct marketing–specific) practice, Lean Startups incorporate it directly into product development.

These changes led to an immediate change in Farb's understanding of the business. Split testing often uncovers surprising things. For example, many features that make the product better in the eyes of engineers and designers have no impact on customer behavior. This was the case at Grockit, as it has been in every company I have seen adopt this technique. Although working with split tests seems to be more difficult because it requires extra accounting and metrics to keep track of each variation, it almost always saves tremendous amounts of time in the long run by eliminating work that doesn't matter to customers.

Split testing also helps teams refine their understanding of what customers want and don't want. Grockit's team constantly added new ways for their customers to interact with each other in the hope that those social communication tools would increase the product's value. Inherent in those efforts was the belief that customers desired more communication during their studying. When split testing revealed that the extra features did not change customer behavior, it called that belief into question.

The questioning inspired the team to seek a deeper understanding of what customers really wanted. They brainstormed new ideas for product experiments that might have more impact. In fact, many of these ideas were not new. They had simply been overlooked because the company was focused on building social tools. As a result, Grockit tested an intensive solo-studying mode, complete with quests and gamelike levels, so that students could have the choice of studying by themselves or with others. Just as in Farb's original classroom, this proved extremely effective. Without the discipline of split testing, the company might not have had this realization. In fact, over time, through dozens of tests, it became clear that the key to student engagement was to offer them a combination of social and solo features. Students preferred having a choice of how to study.

Kanban

Following the lean manufacturing principle of *kanban,* or capacity constraint, Grockit changed the product prioritization process. Under the new system, user stories were not considered complete until they led to validated learning. Thus, stories could be cataloged as being in one of four states of development: in the product backlog, actively being built, done (feature complete from a technical point of view), or in the process of being validated. Validated was defined as "knowing whether the story was a good idea to have been done in the first place." This validation usually would come in the form of a split test showing a change in customer behavior but also might include customer interviews or surveys.

The *kanban* rule permitted only so many stories in each of the four states. As stories flow from one state to the other, the buckets fill up. Once a bucket becomes full, it cannot accept more stories. Only when a story has been validated can it be removed from the *kanban* board. If the validation fails and it turns out the story is a bad idea, the relevant feature is removed from the product (see the chart on page 139).

KANBAN DIAGRAM OF WORK AS IT PROGRESSES FROM STAGE TO STAGE

(No bucket can contain more than three projects at a time.)

BACKLOG	IN PROGRESS	BUILT	VALIDATED
A B C	D E	F	

Work on A begins. D and E are in development. F awaits validation.

BACKLOG	IN PROGRESS	BUILT	VALIDATED
G H I	B C	D E A	F

F is validated. D and E await validation. G, H, I are new tasks to be undertaken. B and C are being built. A completes development.

BACKLOG	IN PROGRESS	BUILT	VALIDATED
H → I →	G B → C →	D E A	F

B and C have been built, but under *kanban,* cannot be moved to the next bucket for validation until A, D, E have been validated. Work cannot begin on H and I until space opens up in the buckets ahead.

I have implemented this system with several teams, and the initial result is always frustrating: each bucket fills up, starting with the "validated" bucket and moving on to the "done" bucket, until it's not possible to start any more work. Teams that are used to measuring their productivity narrowly, by the number of stories they are delivering, feel stuck. The only way to start work on new features is to investigate some of the stories that are done but haven't been validated. That often requires nonengineering efforts: talking to customers, looking at split-test data, and the like.

Pretty soon everyone gets the hang of it. This progress occurs in fits and starts at first. Engineering may finish a big batch of work, followed by extensive testing and validation. As engineers look for ways to increase their productivity, they start to realize that if they include the validation exercise from the beginning, the whole team can be more productive.

For example, why build a new feature that is not part of a split-test experiment? It may save you time in the short run, but it will take more time later to test, during the validation phase. The same logic applies to a story that an engineer doesn't understand. Under the old system, he or she would just build it and find out later what it was for. In the new system, that behavior is clearly counterproductive: without a clear hypothesis, how can a story ever be validated? We saw this behavior at IMVU, too. I once saw a junior engineer face down a senior executive over a relatively minor change. The engineer insisted that the new feature be split-tested, just like any other. His peers backed him up; it was considered absolutely obvious that all features should be routinely tested, no matter who was commissioning them. (Embarrassingly, all too often I was the executive in question.) A solid process lays the foundation for a healthy culture, one where ideas are evaluated by merit and not by job title.

Most important, teams working in this system begin to measure their productivity according to validated learning, not in terms of the production of new features.

Hypothesis Testing at Grockit

When Grockit made this transition, the results were dramatic. In one case, they decided to test one of their major features, called lazy registration, to see if it was worth the heavy investment they were making in ongoing support. They were confident in this feature because lazy registration is considered one of the design best practices for online services. In this system, customers do not have to register for the service up front. Instead, they immediately begin using the service and are asked to register only after they have had a chance to experience the service's benefit.

For a student, lazy registration works like this: when you come to the Grockit website, you're immediately placed in a study session with other students working on the same test. You don't have to give your name, e-mail address, or credit card number. There is nothing to prevent you from jumping in and getting started immediately. For Grockit, this was essential to testing one of its core assumptions: that customers would be willing to adopt this new way of learning only if they could see proof that it was working early on.

As a result of this hypothesis, Grockit's design required that it manage three classes of users: unregistered guests, registered (trial) guests, and customers who had paid for the premium version of the product. This design required significant extra work to build and maintain: the more classes of users there are, the more work is required to keep track of them, and the more marketing effort is required to create the right incentives to entice customers to upgrade to the next class. Grockit had undertaken this extra effort because lazy registration was considered an industry best practice.

I encouraged the team to try a simple split-test. They took

one cohort of customers and required that they register immediately, based on nothing more than Grockit's marketing materials. To their surprise, this cohort's behavior was exactly the same as that of the lazy registration group: they had the same rate of registration, activation, and subsequent retention. In other words, the extra effort of lazy registration was a complete waste even though it was considered an industry best practice.

Even more important than reducing waste was the insight that this test suggested: customers were basing their decision about Grockit on something other than their use of the product.

Think about this. Think about the cohort of customers who were required to register for the product before entering a study session with other students. They had very little information about the product, nothing more than was presented on Grockit's home page and registration page. By contrast, the lazy registration group had a tremendous amount of information about the product because they had used it. Yet despite this information disparity, customer behavior was exactly the same.

This suggested that improving Grockit's positioning and marketing might have a more significant impact on attracting new customers than would adding new features. This was just the first of many important experiments Grockit was able to run. Since those early days, they have expanded their customer base dramatically: they now offer test prep for numerous standardized tests, including the GMAT, SAT, ACT, and GRE, as well as online math and English courses for students in grades 7 through 12.

Grockit continues to evolve its process, seeking continuous improvement at every turn. With more than twenty employees in its San Francisco office, Grockit continues to operate with the same deliberate, disciplined approach that has been their hallmark all along. They have helped close to a million students and are sure to help millions more.

THE VALUE OF THE THREE A'S

These examples from Grockit demonstrate each of the three A's of metrics: actionable, accessible, and auditable.

Actionable

For a report to be considered actionable, it must demonstrate clear cause and effect. Otherwise, it is a vanity metric. The reports that Grockit's team began to use to judge their learning milestones made it extremely clear what actions would be necessary to replicate the results.

By contrast, vanity metrics fail this criterion. Take the number of hits to a company website. Let's say we have 40,000 hits this month—a new record. What do we need to do to get more hits? Well, that depends. Where are the new hits coming from? Is it from 40,000 new customers or from one guy with an extremely active web browser? Are the hits the result of a new marketing campaign or PR push? What is a hit, anyway? Does each page in the browser count as one hit, or do all the embedded images and multimedia content count as well? Those who have sat in a meeting debating the units of measurement in a report will recognize this problem.

Vanity metrics wreak havoc because they prey on a weakness of the human mind. In my experience, when the numbers go up, people think the improvement was caused by their actions, by whatever they were working on at the time. That is why it's so common to have a meeting in which marketing thinks the numbers went up because of a new PR or marketing effort and engineering thinks the better numbers are the result of the new features it added. Finding out what is actually going on is extremely costly, and so most managers simply move on, doing the best they can to form their own judgment on the basis of their experience and the collective intelligence in the room.

Unfortunately, when the numbers go down, it results in a very different reaction: now it's somebody else's fault. Thus, most team members or departments live in a world where their department is constantly making things better, only to have their hard work sabotaged by other departments that just don't get it. Is it any wonder these departments develop their own distinct language, jargon, culture, and defense mechanisms against the bozos working down the hall?

Actionable metrics are the antidote to this problem. When cause and effect is clearly understood, people are better able to learn from their actions. Human beings are innately talented learners when given a clear and objective assessment.

Accessible

All too many reports are not understood by the employees and managers who are supposed to use them to guide their decision making. Unfortunately, most managers do not respond to this complexity by working hand in hand with the data warehousing team to simplify the reports so that they can understand them better. Departments too often spend their energy learning how to use data to get what they want rather than as genuine feedback to guide their future actions.

There is an antidote to this misuse of data. First, make the reports as simple as possible so that everyone understands them. Remember the saying "Metrics are people, too." The easiest way to make reports comprehensible is to use tangible, concrete units. What is a website hit? Nobody is really sure, but everyone knows what a person visiting the website is: one can practically picture those people sitting at their computers.

This is why cohort-based reports are the gold standard of

learning metrics: they turn complex actions into people-based reports. Each cohort analysis says: among the people who used our product in this period, here's how many of them exhibited each of the behaviors we care about. In the IMVU example, we saw four behaviors: downloading the product, logging into the product from one's computer, engaging in a chat with other customers, and upgrading to the paid version of the product. In other words, the report deals with people and their actions, which are far more useful than piles of data points. For example, think about how hard it would have been to tell if IMVU was being successful if we had reported only on the total number of person-to-person conversations. Let's say we have 10,000 conversations in a period. Is that good? Is that one person being very, very social, or is it 10,000 people each trying the product one time and then giving up? There's no way to know without creating a more detailed report.

As the gross numbers get larger, accessibility becomes more and more important. It is hard to visualize what it means if the number of website hits goes down from 250,000 in one month to 200,000 the next month, but most people understand immediately what it means to lose 50,000 customers. That's practically a whole stadium full of people who are abandoning the product.

Accessibility also refers to widespread access to the reports. Grockit did this especially well. Every day their system automatically generated a document containing the latest data for every single one of their split-test experiments and other leap-of-faith metrics. This document was mailed to every employee of the company: they all always had a fresh copy in their e-mail inboxes. The reports were well laid out and easy to read, with each experiment and its results explained in plain English.

Another way to make reports accessible is to use a technique we developed at IMVU. Instead of housing the analytics or data in a separate system, our reporting data and its infrastructure were considered part of the product itself and were owned by the product development team. The reports were available on our website, accessible to anyone with an employee account.

Each employee could log in to the system at any time, choose from a list of all current and past experiments, and see a simple one-page summary of the results. Over time, those one-page summaries became the de facto standard for settling product arguments throughout the organization. When people needed evidence to support something they had learned, they would bring a printout with them to the relevant meeting, confident that everyone they showed it to would understand its meaning.

Auditable

When informed that their pet project is a failure, most of us are tempted to blame the messenger, the data, the manager, the gods, or anything else we can think of. That's why the third A of good metrics, "auditable," is so essential. We must ensure that the data is credible to employees.

The employees at IMVU would brandish one-page reports to demonstrate what they had learned to settle arguments, but the process often wasn't so smooth. Most of the time, when a manager, developer, or team was confronted with results that would kill a pet project, the loser of the argument would challenge the veracity of the data.

Such challenges are more common than most managers would admit, and unfortunately, most data reporting systems are not designed to answer them successfully. Sometimes this is the result of a well-intentioned but misplaced desire to protect the privacy of customers. More often, the lack of such supporting documentation is simply a matter of neglect. Most data reporting systems are not built by product development teams, whose job is to prioritize and build product features. They are built by business managers and analysts. Managers who must use these systems can only check to see if the reports are mutually consistent. They all too often lack a way to test if the data is consistent with reality.

The solution? First, remember that "Metrics are people, too." We need to be able to test the data by hand, in the messy real world, by talking to customers. This is the only way to be able to check if the reports contain true facts. Managers need the ability to spot check the data with real customers. It also has a second benefit: systems that provide this level of auditability give managers and entrepreneurs the opportunity to gain insights into why customers are behaving the way the data indicate.

Second, those building reports must make sure the mechanisms that generate the reports are not too complex. Whenever possible, reports should be drawn directly from the master data, rather than from an intermediate system, which reduces opportunities for error. I have noticed that every time a team has one of its judgments or assumptions overturned as a result of a technical problem with the data, its confidence, morale, and discipline are undermined.

○ ○ ○

When we watch entrepreneurs succeed in the mythmaking world of Hollywood, books, and magazines, the story is always structured the same way. First, we see the plucky protagonist having an epiphany, hatching a great new idea. We learn about his or her character and personality, how he or she came to be in the right place at the right time, and how he or she took the dramatic leap to start a business.

Then the photo montage begins. It's usually short, just a few minutes of time-lapse photography or narrative. We see the protagonist building a team, maybe working in a lab, writing on whiteboards, closing sales, pounding on a few keyboards. At the end of the montage, the founders are successful, and the story can move on to more interesting fare: how to split the spoils of their success, who will appear on magazine covers, who sues whom, and implications for the future.

Unfortunately, the real work that determines the success of startups happens during the photo montage. It doesn't make the cut in terms of the big story because it is too boring. Only 5 percent of entrepreneurship is the big idea, the business model, the whiteboard strategizing, and the splitting up of the spoils. The other 95 percent is the gritty work that is measured by innovation accounting: product prioritization decisions, deciding which customers to target or listen to, and having the courage to subject a grand vision to constant testing and feedback.

One decision stands out above all others as the most difficult, the most time-consuming, and the biggest source of waste for most startups. We all must face this fundamental test: deciding when to pivot and when to persevere. To understand what happens during the photo montage, we have to understand how to pivot, and that is the subject of Chapter 8.

8
PIVOT (OR PERSEVERE)

Every entrepreneur eventually faces an overriding challenge in developing a successful product: deciding when to pivot and when to persevere. Everything that has been discussed so far is a prelude to a seemingly simple question: are we making sufficient progress to believe that our original strategic hypothesis is correct, or do we need to make a major change? That change is called a pivot: a structured course correction designed to test a new fundamental hypothesis about the product, strategy, and engine of growth.

Because of the scientific methodology that underlies the Lean Startup, there is often a misconception that it offers a rigid clinical formula for making pivot or persevere decisions. This is not true. There is no way to remove the human element—vision, intuition, judgment—from the practice of entrepreneurship, nor would that be desirable.

My goal in advocating a scientific approach to the creation of startups is to channel human creativity into its most productive form, and there is no bigger destroyer of creative potential than the misguided decision to persevere. Companies that cannot bring themselves to pivot to a new direction on the basis of feedback from the marketplace can get stuck in the land of the living dead, neither growing enough nor dying, consuming resources and commitment from employees and other stakeholders but not moving ahead.

There is good news about our reliance on judgment, though. We are able to learn, we are innately creative, and we have a remarkable ability to see the signal in the noise. In fact, we are so good at this that sometimes we see signals that aren't there. The heart of the scientific method is the realization that although human judgment may be faulty, we can improve our judgment by subjecting our theories to repeated testing.

Startup productivity is not about cranking out more widgets or features. It is about aligning our efforts with a business and product that are working to create value and drive growth. In other words, successful pivots put us on a path toward growing a sustainable business.

INNOVATION ACCOUNTING LEADS TO FASTER PIVOTS

To see this process in action, meet David Binetti, the CEO of Votizen. David has had a long career helping to bring the American political process into the twenty-first century. In the early 1990s, he helped build USA.gov, the first portal for the federal government. He's also experienced some classic startup failures. When it came time to build Votizen, David was determined to avoid betting the farm on his vision.

David wanted to tackle the problem of civic participation in the political process. His first product concept was a social network of verified voters, a place where people passionate about civic causes could get together, share ideas, and recruit their friends. David built his first minimum viable product for just over $1,200 in about three months and launched it.

David wasn't building something that *nobody* wanted. In fact, from its earliest days, Votizen was able to attract early adopters who loved the core concept. Like all entrepreneurs, David had to refine his product and business model. What made David's challenge especially hard was that he had to make those pivots in the face of moderate success.

David's initial concept involved four big leaps of faith:

1. Customers would be interested enough in the social network to sign up. (Registration)
2. Votizen would be able to verify them as registered voters. (Activation)
3. Customers who were verified voters would engage with the site's activism tools over time. (Retention)
4. Engaged customers would tell their friends about the service and recruit them into civic causes. (Referral)

Three months and $1,200 later, David's first MVP was in customers' hands. In the initial cohorts, 5 percent signed up for the service and 17 percent verified their registered voter status (see the chart below). The numbers were so low that there wasn't enough data to tell what sort of engagement or referral would occur. It was time to start iterating.

	INITIAL MVP
Registration	5%
Activation	17%
Retention	Too low
Referral	Too low

David spent the next two months and another $5,000 split testing new product features, messaging, and improving the product's design to make it easier to use. Those tests showed dramatic improvements, going from a 5 percent registration rate to 17 percent and from a 17 percent activation rate to over 90 percent. Such is the power of split testing. This optimization gave David a critical mass of customers with which to measure the next two leaps of faith. However, as shown in the chart below, those numbers proved to be even more discouraging: David achieved a referral rate of only 4 percent and a retention rate of 5 percent.

	INITIAL MVP	AFTER OPTIMIZATION
Registration	5%	17%
Activation	17%	90%
Retention	Too low	5%
Referral	Too low	4%

David knew he had to do more development and testing. For the next three months he continued to optimize, split test, and refine his pitch. He talked to customers, held focus groups, and did countless A/B experiments. As was explained in Chapter 7, in a split test, different versions of a product are offered to different customers at the same time. By observing the changes in behavior between the two groups, one can make inferences about the impact of the different variations. As shown in the chart below, the referral rate nudged up slightly to 6 percent and the retention rate went up to 8 percent. A disappointed David had spent eight months and $20,000 to build a product that wasn't living up to the growth model he'd hoped for.

	BEFORE OPTIMIZATION	AFTER OPTIMIZATION
Registration	17%	17%
Activation	90%	90%
Retention	5%	8%
Referral	4%	6%

David faced the difficult challenge of deciding whether to pivot or persevere. This is one of the hardest decisions entrepreneurs face. The goal of creating learning milestones is not to make the decision easy; it is to make sure that there is relevant data in the room when it comes time to decide.

Remember, at this point David has had many customer conversations. He has plenty of learning that he can use to rationalize the failure he has experienced with the current product. That's exactly what many entrepreneurs do. In Silicon Valley, we call this experience getting stuck in the land of the living dead. It happens when a company has achieved a modicum of success—just enough to stay alive—but is not living up to the expectations of its founders and investors. Such companies are a terrible drain of human energy. Out of loyalty, the employees and founders don't want to give in; they feel that success might be just around the corner.

David had two advantages that helped him avoid this fate:

1. Despite being committed to a significant vision, he had done his best to launch early and iterate. Thus, he was facing a pivot or persevere moment just eight months into the life of his company. The more money, time, and creative energy that has been sunk into an idea, the harder it is to pivot. David had done well to avoid that trap.
2. David had identified his leap-of-faith questions explicitly at the outset and, more important, had made quantitative predictions about each of them. It would not have been difficult for him to declare success retroactively from that initial venture. After all, some of his metrics, such as activation, were doing quite well. In terms of gross metrics such as total usage, the company had positive growth. It is only because David focused on actionable metrics for each of his leap-of-faith questions that he was able to

accept that his company was failing. In addition, because David had not wasted energy on premature PR, he was able to make this determination without public embarrassment or distraction.

Failure is a prerequisite to learning. The problem with the notion of shipping a product and then seeing what happens is that you are guaranteed to succeed—at seeing what happens. But then what? As soon as you have a handful of customers, you're likely to have five opinions about what to do next. Which should you listen to?

Votizen's results were okay, but they were not good enough. David felt that although his optimization was improving the metrics, they were not trending toward a model that would sustain the business overall. But like all good entrepreneurs, he did not give up prematurely. David decided to pivot and test a new hypothesis. A pivot requires that we keep one foot rooted in what we've learned so far, while making a fundamental change in strategy in order to seek even greater validated learning. In this case, David's direct contact with customers proved essential.

He had heard three recurring bits of feedback in his testing:

1. "I always wanted to get more involved; this makes it so much easier."
2. "The fact that you prove I'm a voter matters."
3. "There's no one here. What's the point of coming back?"[1]

David decided to undertake what I call a *zoom-in pivot*, refocusing the product on what previously had been considered just one feature of a larger whole. Think of the customer comments above: customers like the concept, they like the voter registration technology, but they aren't getting value out of the social networking part of the product.

David decided to change Votizen into a product called @2gov, a "social lobbying platform." Rather than get customers integrated in a civic social network, @2gov allows them to contact their elected representatives quickly and easily via existing social networks such as Twitter. The customer engages digitally, but @2gov translates that digital contact into paper form. Members of Congress receive old-fashioned printed letters and petitions as a result. In other words, @2gov translates the high-tech world of its customers into the low-tech world of politics.

@2gov had a slightly different set of leap-of-faith questions to answer. It still depended on customers signing up, verifying their voter status, and referring their friends, but the growth model changed. Instead of relying on an engagement-driven business ("sticky" growth), @2gov was more transactional. David's hypothesis was that passionate activists would be willing to pay money to have @2gov facilitate contacts on behalf of voters who cared about their issues.

David's new MVP took four months and another $30,000. He'd now spent a grand total of $50,000 and worked for twelve months. But the results from his next round of testing were dramatic: registration rate 42 percent, activation 83 percent, retention 21 percent, and referral a whopping 54 percent. However, the number of activists willing to pay was less than 1 percent. The value of each transaction was far too low to sustain a profitable business even after David had done his best to optimize it.

Before we get to David's next pivot, notice how convincingly he was able to demonstrate validated learning. He hoped that with this new product, he would be able to improve his leap-of-faith metrics dramatically, and he did (see the chart below).

	BEFORE PIVOT	**AFTER PIVOT**
Engine of growth	Sticky	Paid
Registration rate	17%	42%
Activation	90%	83%
Retention	8%	21%
Referral	6%	54%
Revenue	n/a	1%
Lifetime value (LTV)	n/a	Minimal

He did this not by working harder but by working smarter, taking his product development resources and applying them to a new and different product. Compared with the previous four months of optimization, the new four months of pivoting had resulted in a dramatically higher return on investment, but David was still stuck in an age-old entrepreneurial trap. His metrics and product were improving, but not fast enough.

David pivoted again. This time, rather than rely on activists to pay money to drive contacts, he went to large organizations, professional fund-raisers, and big companies, which all have a professional or business interest in political campaigning. The companies seemed extremely eager to use and pay for David's service, and David quickly signed letters of intent to build the functionality they needed. In this pivot, David did what I call a *customer segment pivot*, keeping the functionality of the product the same but changing the audience focus. He focused on who pays: from consumers to businesses and nonprofit organizations. In other words, David went from being a business-to-consumer (B2C) company to being a business-to-business (B2B) company. In the process he changed his planned growth model, as well to one where he would be able to fund growth out of the profits generated from each B2B sale.

Three months later, David had built the functionality he had promised, based on those early letters of intent. But when he went back to companies to collect his checks, he discovered more problems. Company after company procrastinated, delayed, and ultimately passed up the opportunity. Although they had been excited enough to sign a letter of intent, closing a real sale was much more difficult. It turned out that those companies were not early adopters.

On the basis of the letters of intent, David had increased his head count, taking on additional sales staff and engineers in anticipation of having to service higher-margin business-to-business accounts. When the sales didn't materialize, the whole team had to work harder to try to find revenue elsewhere. Yet no matter how many sales calls they went on and no matter how much optimization they did to the product, the model wasn't working. Returning to his leap-of-faith questions, David concluded that the results refuted his business-to-business hypothesis, and so he decided to pivot once again.

All this time, David was learning and gaining feedback from his potential customers, but he was in an unsustainable situation. You can't pay staff with what you've learned, and raising money at that juncture would have escalated the problem. Raising money without early traction is not a certain thing. If he had been able to raise money, he could have kept the company going but would have been pouring money into a value-destroying engine of growth. He would be in a high-pressure situation: use investor's cash to make the engine of growth work or risk having to shut down the company (or be replaced).

David decided to reduce staff and pivot again, this time attempting what I call a *platform pivot*. Instead of selling an application to one customer at a time, David envisioned a new growth model inspired by Google's AdWords platform. He built a self-serve sales platform where anyone could become a customer with just a credit card. Thus, no matter what cause you were passionate about, you could go to @2gov's website and @2gov would help you find new people to get involved. As always, the new people were verified registered voters, and so their opinions carried weight with elected officials.

The new product took only one additional month to build and immediately showed results: 51 percent sign-up rate, 92 percent activation rate, 28 percent retention rate, 64 percent referral rate (see the chart below). Most important, 11 percent of these customers were willing to pay 20 cents per message. Most important, this was the beginning of an actual growth model that could work. Receiving 20 cents per message might not sound like much, but the high referral rate meant that @2gov could grow its traffic without spending significant marketing money (this is the viral engine of growth).

	BEFORE PIVOT	**AFTER PIVOT**
Engine of growth	Paid	Viral
Registration rate	42%	51%
Activation	83%	92%
Retention	21%	28%
Referral	54%	64%
Revenue	1%	11%
Lifetime value (LTV)	Minimal	$0.20 per message

Votizen's story exhibits some common patterns. One of the most important to note is the acceleration of MVPs. The first MVP took eight months, the next four months, then three, then one. Each time David was able to validate or refute his next hypothesis faster than before.

How can one explain this acceleration? It is tempting to credit it to the product development work that had been going on. Many features had been created, and with them a fair amount of infrastructure. Therefore, each time the company pivoted, it didn't have to start from scratch. But this is not the whole story. For one thing, much of the product had to be discarded between pivots. Worse, the product that remained was classified as a legacy product, one that was no longer suited to the goals of the company. As is usually the case, the effort required to reform a legacy product took extra work. Counteracting these forces were the hard-won lessons David had learned through each milestone. Votizen accelerated its MVP process because it was learning critical things about its customers, market, and strategy.

Today, two years after its inception, Votizen is doing well. They recently raised $1.5 million from Facebook's initial investor Peter Thiel, one of the very few consumer Internet investments he has made in recent years. Votizen's system now can process voter identity in real time for forty-seven states representing 94 percent of the U.S. population and has delivered tens of thousands of messages to Congress. The Startup Visa campaign used Votizen's tools to introduce the Startup Visa Act (S.565), which is the first legislation introduced into the Senate solely as a result of social lobbying. These activities have attracted the attention of established Washington consultants who are seeking to employ Votizen's tools in future political campaigns.

David Binetti sums up his experience building a Lean Startup:

> In 2003 I started a company in roughly the same space as I'm in today. I had roughly the same domain expertise and industry credibility, fresh off the USA.gov success. But back then my company was a total failure (despite

consuming significantly greater investment), while now I have a business making money and closing deals. Back then I did the traditional linear product development model, releasing an amazing product (it really was) after 12 months of development, only to find that no one would buy it. This time I produced four versions in twelve weeks and generated my first sale relatively soon after that. And it isn't just market timing—two other companies that launched in a similar space in 2003 subsequently sold for tens of millions of dollars, and others in 2010 followed a linear model straight to the dead pool.

A STARTUP'S RUNWAY IS THE NUMBER OF PIVOTS IT CAN STILL MAKE

Seasoned entrepreneurs often speak of the runway that their startup has left: the amount of time remaining in which a startup must either achieve lift-off or fail. This usually is defined as the remaining cash in the bank divided by the monthly burn rate, or net drain on that account balance. For example, a startup with $1 million in the bank that is spending $100,000 per month has a projected runway of ten months.

When startups start to run low on cash, they can extend the runway two ways: by cutting costs or by raising additional funds. But when entrepreneurs cut costs indiscriminately, they are as liable to cut the costs that are allowing the company to get through its Build-Measure-Learn feedback loop as they are to cut waste. If the cuts result in a slowdown to this feedback loop, all they have accomplished is to help the startup go out of business more slowly.

The true measure of runway is how many pivots a startup has left: the number of opportunities it has to make a fundamental change to its business strategy. Measuring runway through the lens of pivots rather than that of time suggests another way to extend that runway: get to each pivot faster. In other words, the startup has to find ways to achieve the same amount of validated learning at lower cost or in a shorter time. All the techniques in the Lean Startup model that have been discussed so far have this as their overarching goal.

PIVOTS REQUIRE COURAGE

Ask most entrepreneurs who have decided to pivot and they will tell you that they wish they had made the decision sooner. I believe there are three reasons why this happens.

First, vanity metrics can allow entrepreneurs to form false conclusions and live in their own private reality. This is particularly damaging to the decision to pivot because it robs teams of the belief that it is necessary to change. When people are forced to change against their better judgment, the process is harder, takes longer, and leads to a less decisive outcome.

Second, when an entrepreneur has an unclear hypothesis, it's almost impossible to experience complete failure, and without failure there is usually no impetus to embark on the radical change a pivot requires. As I mentioned earlier, the failure of the "launch it and see what happens" approach should now be evident: you will always succeed—in seeing what happens. Except in rare cases, the early results will be ambiguous, and you won't know whether to pivot or persevere, whether to change direction or stay the course.

Third, many entrepreneurs are afraid. Acknowledging failure can lead to dangerously low morale. Most entrepreneurs' biggest fear is not that their vision will prove to be wrong. More terrifying is the thought that the vision might be deemed wrong without having been given a real chance to prove itself. This fear drives much of the resistance to the minimum viable product, split testing, and other techniques to test hypotheses. Ironically, this fear drives up the risk because testing doesn't occur until the vision is fully represented. However, by that time it is often too late to pivot because funding is running out. To avoid this fate, entrepreneurs need to face their fears and be willing to fail, often in a public way. In fact, entrepreneurs who have a high profile, either because of personal fame or because they are operating as part of a famous brand, face an extreme version of this problem.

A new startup in Silicon Valley called Path was started by experienced entrepreneurs: Dave Morin, who previously had overseen Facebook's platform initiative; Dustin Mierau, product designer and cocreator of Macster; and Shawn Fanning of Napster fame. They decided to release a minimum viable product in 2010. Because of the high-profile nature of its founders, the MVP attracted significant press attention, especially from technology and startup blogs. Unfortunately, their product was not targeted at technology early adopters, and as a result, the early blogger reaction was quite negative. (Many entrepreneurs fail to launch because they are afraid of this kind of reaction, worrying that it will harm the morale of the entire company. The allure of positive press, especially in our "home" industry, is quite strong.)

Luckily, the Path team had the courage to ignore this fear and focus on what their customers said. As a result, they were able to get essential early feedback from actual customers. Path's goal is to create a more personal social network that maintains its quality over time. Many people have had the experience of being overconnected on existing social networks, sharing with past coworkers, high school friends, relatives, and colleagues. Such broad groups make it hard to share intimate moments. Path took an unusual approach. For example, it limited the number of connections to fifty, based on brain research by the anthropologist Robin Dunbar at Oxford. His research suggests that fifty is roughly the number of personal relationships in any person's life at any given time.

For members of the tech press (and many tech early adopters) this "artificial" constraint on the number of connections was anathema. They routinely use new social networking products with thousands of connections. Fifty seemed way too small. As a result, Path endured a lot of public criticism, which was hard to ignore. But customers flocked to the platform, and their feedback was decidedly different from the negativity in the press. Customers liked the intimate moments and consistently wanted features that were not on the original product road map, such as the ability to share how friends' pictures made them feel and the ability to share "video moments."

Dave Morin summed up his experience this way:

> The reality of our team and our backgrounds built up a massive wall of expectations. I don't think it would have mattered what we would have released; we would have been met with expectations that are hard to live up to. But to us it just meant we needed to get our product and our vision out into the market broadly in order to get feedback and to begin iteration. We humbly test our theories and our approach to see what the market thinks. Listen to feedback honestly. And continue to innovate in the directions we think will create meaning in the world.

Path's story is just beginning, but already their courage in facing down critics is paying off. If and when they need to pivot, they won't be hampered by fear. They recently raised $8.5 million in venture capital in a round led by Kleiner Perkins Caufield & Byers. In doing so, Path reportedly turned down an acquisition offer for $100 million from Google.[2]

THE PIVOT OR PERSEVERE MEETING

The decision to pivot requires a clear-eyed and objective mind-set. We've discussed the telltale signs of the need to pivot: the decreasing effectiveness of product experiments and the general feeling that product development should be more productive. Whenever you see those symptoms, consider a pivot.

The decision to pivot is emotionally charged for any startup and has to be addressed in a structured way. One way to mitigate this challenge is to schedule the meeting in advance. I recommend that every startup have a regular "pivot or persevere" meeting. In my experience, less than a few weeks between meetings is too often and more than a few months is too infrequent. However, each startup needs to find its own pace.

Each pivot or persevere meeting requires the participation of both the product development and business leadership teams. At IMVU, we also added the perspectives of outside advisers who could help us see past our preconceptions and interpret data in new ways. The product development team must bring a complete report of the results of its product optimization efforts over time (not just the past period) as well as a comparison of how those results stack up against expectations (again, over time). The business leadership should bring detailed accounts of their conversations with current and potential customers.

Let's take a look at this process in action in a dramatic pivot done by a company called Wealthfront. That company was founded in 2007 by Dan Carroll and added Andy Rachleff as CEO shortly thereafter. Andy is a well-known figure in Silicon Valley: he is a cofounder and former general partner of the venture capital firm Benchmark Capital and is on the faculty of the Stanford Graduate School of Business, where he teaches a variety of courses on technology entrepreneurship. I first met Andy when he commissioned a case study on IMVU to teach his students about the process we had used to build the company.

Wealthfront's mission is to disrupt the mutual fund industry by bringing greater transparency, access, and value to retail investors. What makes Wealthfront's story unusual, however, is not where it is today but how it began: as an online game.

In Wealthfront's original incarnation it was called kaChing and was conceived as a kind of fantasy league for amateur investors. It allowed anyone to open a virtual trading account and build a portfolio that was based on real market data without having to invest real money. The idea was to identify diamonds in the rough: amateur traders who lacked the resources to become fund managers but who possessed market insight. Wealthfront's founders did not want to be in the online gaming business per se; kaChing was part of a sophisticated strategy in the service of their larger vision. Any student of disruptive innovation would have looked on approvingly: they were following that system perfectly by initially serving customers who were unable to participate in the mainstream market. Over time, they believed, the product would become more and more sophisticated, eventually allowing users to serve (and disrupt) existing professional fund managers.

To identify the best amateur trading savants, Wealthfront built sophisticated technology to rate the skill of each fund manager, using techniques employed by the most sophisticated evaluators of money managers, the premier U.S. university endowments. Those methods allowed them to evaluate not just the returns the managers generated but also the amount of risk they had taken along with how consistent they performed relative to their declared investment strategy. Thus, fund managers who achieved great returns through reckless gambles (i.e., investments outside their area of expertise) would be ranked lower than those who had figured out how to beat the market through skill.

With its kaChing game, Wealthfront hoped to test two leap-of-faith assumptions:

1. A significant percentage of the game players would demonstrate enough talent as virtual fund managers to prove themselves suitable to become managers of real assets (the value hypothesis).
2. The game would grow using the viral engine of growth and generate value using a freemium business model. The game was free to play, but the team hoped that a percentage of the players would realize that they were lousy traders and therefore want to convert to paying customers once Wealthfront started offering real asset management services (the growth hypothesis).

kaChing was a huge early success, attracting more than 450,000 gamers in its initial launch. By now, you should be suspicious of this kind of vanity metric. Many less disciplined companies would have celebrated that success and felt their future was secure, but Wealthfront had identified its assumptions clearly and was able to think more rigorously. By the time Wealthfront was ready to launch its paid financial product, only seven amateur managers had qualified as worthy of managing other people's money, far less than the ideal model had anticipated. After the paid product launched, they were able to measure the conversion rate of gamers into paying customers. Here too the numbers were discouraging: the conversion rate was close to zero. Their model had predicted that hundreds of customers would sign up, but only fourteen did.

The team worked valiantly to find ways to improve the product, but none showed any particular promise. It was time for a pivot or persevere meeting.

If the data we have discussed so far was all that was available at that critical meeting, Wealthfront would have been in trouble. They would have known that their current strategy wasn't working but not what to do to fix it. That is why it was critical that they followed the recommendation earlier in this chapter to investigate alternative possibilities. In this case, Wealthfront had pursued two important lines of inquiry.

The first was a series of conversations with professional money managers, beginning with John Powers, the head of Stanford University's endowment, who reacted surprisingly positively. Wealthfront's strategy was premised on the assumption that professional money managers would be reluctant to join the system because the increased transparency would threaten their sense of authority. Powers had no such concerns. CEO Andy Rachleff then began a series of conversations with other professional investment managers and brought the results back to the company. His insights were as follows:

1. Successful professional money managers felt they had nothing to fear from transparency, since they believed it would validate their skills.
2. Money managers faced significant challenges in managing and scaling their own businesses. They were hampered by the difficulty of servicing their own accounts and therefore had to require high minimum investments as a way to screen new clients.

The second problem was so severe that Wealthfront was fielding cold calls from professional managers asking out of the blue to join the platform. These were classic early adopters who had the vision to see past the current product to something they could use to achieve a competitive advantage.

The second critical qualitative information came out of conversations with consumers. It turned out that they found the blending of virtual and real portfolio management on the kaChing website confusing. Far from being a clever way of acquiring customers, the freemium strategy was getting in the way by promoting confusion about the company's positioning.

This data informed the pivot or persevere meeting. With everyone present, the team debated what to do with its future. The current strategy wasn't working, but many employees were nervous about abandoning the online game. After all, it was an important part of what they had signed on to build. They had invested significant time and energy building and supporting those customers. It was painful—as it always is—to realize that that energy had been wasted.

Wealthfront decided it could not persevere as it existed. The company chose instead to celebrate what it had learned. If it had not launched its current product, the team never would have learned what it needed to know to pivot. In fact, the experience taught them something essential about their vision. As Andy says, "What we really wanted to change was not who manages the money but who has access to the best possible talent. We'd originally thought we'd need to build a significant business with amateur managers to get professionals to come on board, but fortunately it turns out that wasn't necessary."

The company pivoted, abandoning the gaming customers altogether and focusing on providing a service that allowed customers to invest with professional managers. On the surface, the pivot seems quite dramatic in that the company changed its positioning, its name, and its partner strategy. It even jettisoned a large proportion of the features it had built. But at its core, a surprising amount stayed the same. The most valuable work the company had done was building technology to evaluate managers' effectiveness, and this became the kernel around which the new business was built. This is also common with pivots; it is not necessary to throw out everything that came before and start over. Instead, it's about repurposing what has been built and what has been learned to find a more positive direction.

Today, Wealthfront is prospering as a result of its pivot, with over $180 million invested on the platform and more than forty professional managers.[3] It recently was named one of *Fast Company*'s ten most innovative companies in finance.[4] The company continues to operate with agility, scaling in line with the growth principles outlined in Chapter 12. Wealthfront is also a leading advocate of the development technique known as continuous deployment, which we'll discuss in Chapter 9.

FAILURE TO PIVOT

The decision to pivot is so difficult that many companies fail to make it. I wish I could say that every time I was confronted with the need to pivot, I handled it well, but this is far from true. I remember one failure to pivot especially well.

A few years after IMVU's founding, the company was having tremendous success. The business had grown to over $1 million per month in revenue; we had created more than twenty million avatars for our customers. We managed to raise significant new rounds of financing, and like the global economy, we were riding high. But danger lurked around the corner.

Unknowingly, we had fallen into a classic startup trap. We had been so successful with our early efforts that we were ignoring the principles behind them. As a result, we missed the need to pivot even as it stared us in the face.

We had built an organization that excelled at the kinds of

activities described in earlier chapters: creating minimum viable products to test new ideas and running experiments to tune the engine of growth. Before we had begun to enjoy success, many people had advised against our "low-quality" minimum viable product and experimental approach, urging us to slow down. They wanted us to do things right and focus on quality instead of speed. We ignored that advice, mostly because we wanted to claim the advantages of speed. After our approach was vindicated, the advice we received changed. Now most of the advice we heard was that "you can't argue with success," urging us to stay the course. We liked this advice better, but it was equally wrong.

Remember that the rationale for building low-quality MVPs is that developing any features beyond what early adopters require is a form of waste. However, the logic of this takes you only so far. Once you have found success with early adopters, you want to sell to mainstream customers. Mainstream customers have different requirements and are much more demanding.

The kind of pivot we needed is called a customer segment pivot. In this pivot, the company realizes that the product it's building solves a real problem for real customers but that they are not the customers it originally planned to serve. In other words, the product hypothesis is confirmed only partially. (This chapter described such a pivot in the Votizen story, above.)

A customer segment pivot is an especially tricky pivot to execute because, as we learned the hard way at IMVU, the very actions that made us successful with early adopters were diametrically opposed to the actions we'd have to master to be successful with mainstream customers. We lacked a clear understanding of how our engine of growth operated. We had begun to trust our vanity metrics. We had stopped using learning milestones to hold ourselves accountable. Instead, it was much more convenient to focus on the ever-larger gross metrics that were so exciting: breaking new records in signing up paying customers and active users, monitoring our customer retention rate—you name it. Under the surface, it should have been clear that our efforts at tuning the engine were reaching diminishing returns, the classic sign of the need to pivot.

For example, we spent months trying to improve the product's activation rate (the rate at which new customers become active consumers of the product), which remained stubbornly low. We did countless experiments: usability improvements, new persuasion techniques, incentive programs, customer quests, and other game-like features. Individually, many of these new features and new marketing tools were successful. We measured them rigorously, using A/B experimentation. But taken in aggregate, over the course of many months, we were seeing negligible changes in the overall drivers of our engine of growth. Even our activation rate, which had been the center of our focus, edged up only a few percentage points.

We ignored the signs because the company was still growing, delivering month after month of "up and to the right" results. But we were quickly exhausting our early adopter market. It was getting harder and harder to find customers we could acquire at the prices we were accustomed to paying. As we drove our marketing team to find more customers, they were forced to reach out more to mainstream customers, but mainstream customers are less forgiving of an early product. The activation and monetization rates of new customers started to go down, driving up the cost of acquiring new customers. Pretty soon, our growth was flatlining and our engine sputtered and stalled.

It took us far too long to make the changes necessary to fix this situation. As with all pivots, we had to get back to basics and start the innovation accounting cycle over. It felt like the company's second founding. We had gotten really good at optimizing, tuning, and iterating, but in the process we had lost sight of the purpose of those activities: testing a clear hypothesis in the service of the company's vision. Instead, we were chasing growth, revenue, and profits wherever we could find them.

We needed to reacquaint ourselves with our new mainstream customers. Our interaction designers led the way by developing a clear customer archetype that was based on extensive in-person conversations and observation. Next, we needed to invest heavily in a major product overhaul designed to make the product dramatically easier to use. Because of our overfocus on fine-tuning, we had stopped making large investments like these, preferring to invest in lower-risk and lower-yield testing experiments.

However, investing in quality, design, and larger projects did not require that we abandon our experimental roots. On the contrary, once we realized our mistake and executed the pivot, those skills served us well. We created a sandbox for experimentation like the one described in Chapter 12 and had a cross-functional team work exclusively on this major redesign. As they built, they continuously tested their new design head to head against the old one. Initially, the new design performed worse than the old one, as is usually the case. It lacked the features and functionality of the old design and had many new mistakes as well. But the team relentlessly improved the design until, months later, it performed better. This new design laid the foundation for our future growth.

This foundation has paid off handsomely. By 2009, revenue had more than doubled to over $25 million annually. But we might have enjoyed that success earlier if we had pivoted sooner.[5]

A CATALOG OF PIVOTS

Pivots come in different flavors. The word *pivot* sometimes is used incorrectly as a synonym for *change*. A pivot is a special kind of change designed to test a new fundamental hypothesis about the product, business model, and engine of growth.

Zoom-in Pivot

In this case, what previously was considered a single feature in a product becomes the whole product. This is the type of pivot Votizen made when it pivoted away from a full social network and toward a simple voter contact product.

Zoom-out Pivot

In the reverse situation, sometimes a single feature is insufficient to support a whole product. In this type of pivot, what was considered the whole product becomes a single feature of a much larger product.

Customer Segment Pivot

In this pivot, the company realizes that the product it is building solves a real problem for real customers but that they are not the type of customers it originally planned to serve. In other words, the product hypothesis is partially confirmed, solving the right problem, but for a different customer than originally anticipated.

Customer Need Pivot

As a result of getting to know customers extremely well, it sometimes becomes clear that the problem we're trying to solve for them is not very important. However, because of this customer intimacy, we often discover other related problems that are important and can be solved by our team. In many cases, these related problems may require little more than repositioning the existing product. In other cases, it may require a completely new product. Again, this a case where the product hypothesis is partially confirmed; the target customer has a problem worth solving, just not the one that was originally anticipated.

A famous example is the chain Potbelly Sandwich Shop, which today has over two hundred stores. It began as an antique store in 1977; the owners started to sell sandwiches as a way to bolster traffic to their stores. Pretty soon they had pivoted their way into an entirely different line of business.

Platform Pivot

A platform pivot refers to a change from an application to a platform or vice versa. Most commonly, startups that aspire to create a new platform begin life by selling a single application, the so-called killer app, for their platform. Only later does the platform emerge as a vehicle for third parties to leverage as a way to create their own related products. However, this order is not always set in stone, and some companies have to execute this pivot multiple times.

Business Architecture Pivot

This pivot borrows a concept from Geoffrey Moore, who observed that companies generally follow one of two major business architectures: high margin, low volume (complex systems model) or low margin, high volume (volume operations model).[6] The former commonly is associated with business to business (B2B) or enterprise sales cycles, and the latter with consumer products (there are notable exceptions). In a business architecture pivot, a startup switches architectures. Some companies change from high margin, low volume by going mass market (e.g., Google's search "appliance"); others, originally designed for the mass market, turned out to require long and expensive sales cycles.

Value Capture Pivot

There are many ways to capture the value a company creates. These methods are referred to commonly as monetization or revenue models. These terms are much too limiting. Implicit in the idea of monetization is that it is a separate "feature" of a product that can be added or removed at will. In reality, capturing value is an intrinsic part of the product hypothesis. Often, changes to the way a company captures value can have far-reaching consequences for the rest of the business, product, and marketing strategies.

Engine of Growth Pivot

As we'll see in Chapter 10, there are three primary engines of growth that power startups: the viral, sticky, and paid growth models. In this type of pivot, a company changes its growth strategy to seek faster or more profitable growth. Commonly but not always, the engine of growth also requires a change in the way value is captured.

Channel Pivot

In traditional sales terminology, the mechanism by which a company delivers its product to customers is called the sales channel or distribution channel. For example, consumer packaged goods are sold in a grocery store, cars are sold in dealerships, and much enterprise software is sold (with extensive customization) by consulting and professional services firms. Often, the requirements of the channel determine the price, features, and competitive landscape of a product. A channel pivot is a recognition that the same basic solution could be delivered through a different channel with greater effectiveness. Whenever a company abandons a previously complex sales process to "sell direct" to its end users, a channel pivot is in progress.

It is precisely because of its destructive effect on sales channels that the Internet has had such a disruptive influence in industries that previously required complex sales and distribution channels, such as newspaper, magazine, and book publishing.

Technology Pivot

Occasionally, a company discovers a way to achieve the same solution by using a completely different technology. Technology pivots are much more common in established businesses. In other words, they are a sustaining innovation, an incremental improvement designed to appeal to and retain an existing customer base. Established companies excel at this kind of pivot because so much is not changing. The customer segment is the same, the customer's problem is the same, the value-capture model is the same, and the channel partners are the same. The only question is whether the new technology can provide superior price and/or performance compared with the existing technology.

A PIVOT IS A STRATEGIC HYPOTHESIS

Although the pivots identified above will be familiar to students of business strategy, the ability to pivot is no substitute for sound strategic thinking. The problem with providing famous examples of pivots is that most people are familiar only with the successful end strategies of famous companies. Most readers know that Southwest or Walmart is an example of a low-cost disruption in their markets, that Microsoft an example of a platform monopoly, and that Starbucks has leveraged a powerful premium brand. What is generally less well known are the pivots that were required to discover those strategies. Companies have a strong incentive to align their PR stories around the heroic founder and make it seem that their success was the inevitable result of a good idea.

Thus, although startups often pivot into a strategy that seems similar to that of a successful company, it is important not to put too much stock in these analogies. It's extremely difficult to know if the analogy has been drawn properly. Have we copied the essential features or just superficial ones? Will what worked in that industry work in ours? Will what has worked in the past work today? A pivot is better understood as a new strategic hypothesis that will require a new minimum viable product to test.

Pivots are a permanent fact of life for any growing business. Even after a company achieves initial success, it must continue to pivot. Those familiar with the technology life cycle ideas of theorists such as Geoffrey Moore know certain later-stage pivots by the names he has given them: the Chasm, the Tornado, the Bowling Alley. Readers of the disruptive innovation literature spearheaded by Harvard's Clayton Christensen will be familiar with established companies that fail to pivot when they should. The critical skill for managers today is to match those theories to their present situation so that they apply the right advice at the right time.

Modern managers cannot have escaped the deluge of recent books calling on them to adapt, change, reinvent, or upend their existing businesses. Many of the works in this category are long on exhortations and short on specifics.

A pivot is not just an exhortation to change. Remember, it is a special kind of structured change designed to test a new fundamental hypothesis about the product, business model, and engine of growth. It is the heart of the Lean Startup method. It is what makes the companies that follow Lean Startup resilient in the face of mistakes: if we take a wrong turn, we have the tools we need to realize it and the agility to find another path.

○ ○ ○

In Part Two, we have looked at a startup idea from its initial leaps of faith, tested it with a minimum viable product, used innovation accounting and actionable metrics to evaluate the results, and made the decision to pivot or persevere.

I have treated these subjects in great detail to prepare for what comes next. On the page, these processes may seem clinical, slow, and simple. In the real world, something different is needed. We have learned to steer when moving slowly. Now we must learn to race. Laying a solid foundation is only the first step toward our real destination: acceleration.

Part Three
ACCELERATE

Start Your Engines

Most of the decisions startups face are not clear-cut. How often should you release a product? Is there a reason to release weekly rather than daily or quarterly or annually? Product releases incur overhead, and so from an efficiency point of view, releasing often leaves less time to devote to building the product. However, waiting too long to release can lead to the ultimate waste: making something that nobody wants.

How much time and energy should companies invest in infrastructure and planning early on in *anticipation* of success? Spend too much and you waste precious time that could have been spent learning. Spend too little and you may fail to take advantage of early success and cede market leadership to a fast follower.

What should employees spend their days doing? How do we hold people accountable for learning at an organizational level? Traditional departments create incentive structures that keep people focused on excellence in their specialties: marketing, sales, product development. But what if the company's best interests are served by cross-functional collaboration? Startups need organizational structures that combat the extreme uncertainty that is a startup's chief enemy.

The lean manufacturing movement faced similar questions on the factory floor. Their answers are relevant for startups as well, with some modifications.

The critical first question for any lean transformation is: which activities create value and which are a form of waste? Once you understand this distinction, you can begin using lean techniques to drive out waste and increase the efficiency of the value-creating activities. For these techniques to be used in a startup, they must be adapted to the unique circumstances of entrepreneurship. Recall from Chapter 3 that value in a startup is not the creation of stuff, but rather validated learning about how to build a sustainable business. What products do customers really want? How will our business grow? Who is our customer? Which customers should we listen to and which should we ignore? These are the questions that need answering as quickly as possible to maximize a startup's chances of success. That is what creates value for a startup.

In Part Three, we will develop techniques that allow Lean Startups to grow without sacrificing the speed and agility that are the lifeblood of every startup. Contrary to common belief, lethargy and bureaucracy are not the inevitable fate of companies as they achieve maturity. I believe that with the proper foundation, Lean Startups can grow to become lean enterprises that maintain their agility, learning orientation, and culture of innovation even as they scale.

In Chapter 9, we will see how Lean Startups take advantage of the counterintuitive power of small batches. Just as lean manufacturing has pursued a just-in-time approach to building products, reducing the need for in-process inventory, Lean Startups practice *just-in-time scalability*, conducting product experiments without making massive up-front investments in planning and design.

Chapter 10 will explore the metrics startups should use to understand their growth as they add new customers and discover new markets. Sustainable growth follows one of three engines of growth: paid, viral, or sticky. By identifying which engine of growth a startup is using, it can then direct energy where it will be most effective in growing the business. Each engine requires a focus on unique metrics to evaluate the success of new products and prioritize new experiments. When used with the innovation accounting method described in Part Two, these metrics allow startups to figure out when their growth is at risk of running out and pivot accordingly.

Chapter 11 shows how to build an *adaptive organization* by investing in the right amount of process to keep teams nimble as they grow. We will see how techniques from the tool kit of lean manufacturing, such as the Five Whys, help startup teams grow without becoming bureaucratic or dysfunctional. We also will see how lean disciplines set the stage for a startup to transition into an established company driven by operational excellence.

In Chapter 12, we'll come full circle. As startups grow into established companies, they face the same pressures that make it necessary for today's enterprises to find new ways to invest in disruptive innovation. In fact, we'll see that an advantage of a successful startup's rapid growth is that the company can keep its entrepreneurial DNA even as it matures. Today's companies must learn to master a management portfolio of sustainable *and* disruptive innovation. It is an obsolete view that sees startups as going through discrete phases that leave earlier kinds of work—such as innovation—behind. Rather, modern companies must excel at doing multiple kinds of work in parallel. To do so, we'll explore techniques for incubating innovation teams within the context of an established company.

I have included an epilogue called "Waste Not" in which I consider some of the broader implications of the success of the Lean Startup movement, place it in historical context (including cautionary lessons from past movements), and make suggestions for its future direction.

9
BATCH

In the book *Lean Thinking*, James Womack and Daniel Jones recount a story of stuffing newsletters into envelopes with the assistance of one of the author's two young children. Every envelope had to be addressed, stamped, filled with a letter, and sealed. The daughters, age six and nine, knew how they should go about completing the project: "Daddy, first you should fold all of the newsletters. Then you should attach the seal. Then you should put on the stamps." Their father wanted to do it the counterintuitive way: complete each envelope one at a time. They—like most of us—thought that was backward, explaining to him "that wouldn't be efficient!" He and his daughters each took half the envelopes and competed to see who would finish first.

The father won the race, and not just because he is an adult. It happened because the one envelope at a time approach is a faster way of getting the job done even though it seems inefficient. This has been confirmed in many studies, including one that was recorded on video.[1]

The one envelope at a time approach is called "single-piece flow" in lean manufacturing. It works because of the surprising power of small batches. When we do work that proceeds in stages, the "batch size" refers to how much work moves from one stage to the next at a time. For example, if we were stuffing one hundred envelopes, the intuitive way to do it—folding one hundred letters at a time—would have a batch size of one hundred. Single-piece flow is so named because it has a batch size of one.

Why does stuffing one envelope at a time get the job done faster even though it seems like it would be slower? Because our intuition doesn't take into account the extra time required to sort, stack, and move around the large piles of half-complete envelopes when it's done the other way.[2] It seems more efficient to repeat the same task over and over, in part because we expect that we will get better at this simple task the more we do it. Unfortunately, in process-oriented work like this, individual performance is not nearly as important as the overall performance of the system.

Even if the amount of time that each process took was exactly the same, the small batch production approach still would be superior, and for even more counterintuitive reasons. For example, imagine that the letters didn't fit in the envelopes. With the large-batch approach, we wouldn't find that out until nearly the end. With small batches, we'd know almost immediately. What if the envelopes are defective and won't seal? In the large-batch approach, we'd have to unstuff all the envelopes, get new ones, and restuff them. In the small-batch approach, we'd find this out immediately and have no rework required.

All these issues are visible in a process as simple as stuffing envelopes, but they are of real and much greater consequence in the work of every company, large or small. The small-batch approach produces a finished product every few seconds, whereas the large-batch approach must deliver all the products at once, at the end. Imagine what this might look like if the time horizon was hours, days, or weeks. What if it turns out that the customers have decided they don't want the product? Which process would allow a company to find this out sooner?

Lean manufacturers discovered the benefits of small batches decades ago. In the post–World War II economy, Japanese carmakers such as Toyota could not compete with huge American factories that used the latest mass production techniques. Following the intuitively efficient way of building, mass production factories built cars by using ever-larger batch sizes. They would spend huge amounts of money buying machines that could produce car parts by the tens, hundreds, or thousands. By keeping those machines running at peak speed, they could drive down the unit cost of each part and produce cars that were incredibly inexpensive so long as they were completely uniform.

The Japanese car market was far too small for companies such as Toyota to employ those economies of scale; thus, Japanese companies faced intense pressure from mass production. Also, in the war-ravaged Japanese economy, capital was not available for massive investments in large machines.

It was against this backdrop that innovators such as Taiichi Ohno, Shigeo Shingo, and others found a way to succeed by using small batches. Instead of buying large specialized machines that could produce thousands of parts at a time, Toyota used smaller general-purpose machines that could produce a wide variety of parts in small batches. This required figuring out ways to reconfigure each machine rapidly to make the right part at the right time. By focusing on this "changeover time," Toyota was able to produce entire automobiles by using small batches throughout the process.

This rapid changing of machines was no easy feat. As in any lean transformation, existing systems and tools often need to be reinvented to support working in smaller batches. Shigeo Shingo created the concept of SMED (Single-Minute Exchange of Die) in order to enable a smaller batch size of work in early Toyota factories. He was so relentless in rethinking the way machines were operated that he was able to reduce changeover times that previously took hours to less than ten minutes. He did this, not by asking workers to work faster, but by reimagining and restructuring the work that needed to be done. Every investment in better tools and process had a corresponding benefit in terms of shrinking the batch size of work.

Because of its smaller batch size, Toyota was able to produce a much greater diversity of products. It was no longer necessary that each product be exactly the same to gain the economies of scale that powered mass production. Thus, Toyota could serve its smaller, more fragmented markets and still compete with the mass producers. Over time, that capability allowed Toyota to move successfully into larger and larger markets until it became the world's largest automaker in 2008.

The biggest advantage of working in small batches is that quality problems can be identified much sooner. This is the origin of Toyota's famous *andon* cord, which allows any worker to ask for help as soon as they notice any problem, such as a defect in a physical part, stopping the entire production line if it cannot be corrected immediately. This is another very counterintuitive practice. An assembly line works best when it is functioning smoothly, rolling car after car off the end of the line. The *andon* cord can interrupt this careful flow as the line is halted repeatedly. However, the benefits of finding and fixing problems faster outweigh this cost. This process of continuously driving out defects has been a win-win for Toyota and its customers. It is the root cause of Toyota's historic high quality ratings and low costs.

SMALL BATCHES IN ENTREPRENEURSHIP

When I teach entrepreneurs this method, I often begin with stories about manufacturing. Before long, I can see the questioning looks: what does this have to do with my startup? The theory that is the foundation of Toyota's success can be used to dramatically improve the speed at which startups find validated learning.

Toyota discovered that small batches made their factories more efficient. In contrast, in the Lean Startup the goal is not to produce more stuff efficiently. It is to—as quickly as possible—learn how to build a sustainable business.

Think back to the example of envelope stuffing. What if it turns out that the customer doesn't want the product we're building? Although this is never good news for an entrepreneur, finding out sooner is much better than finding out later. Working in small batches ensures that a startup can minimize the expenditure of time, money, and effort that ultimately turns out to have been wasted.

Small Batches at IMVU

At IMVU, we applied these lessons from manufacturing to the way we work. Normally, new versions of products like ours are released to customers on a monthly, quarterly, or yearly cycle.

Take a look at your cell phone. Odds are, it is not the very first version of its kind. Even innovative companies such as Apple produce a new version of their flagship phones about once a year. Bundled up in that product release are dozens of new features (at the release of iPhone 4, Apple boasted more than 1,500 changes).

Ironically, many high-tech products are manufactured in advanced facilities that follow the latest in lean thinking, including small batches and single-piece flow. However, the process that is used to design the product is stuck in the era of mass production. Think of all the changes that are made to a product such as the iPhone; all 1,500 of them are released to customers in one giant batch.

Behind the scenes, in the development and design of the product itself, large batches are still the rule. The work that goes into the development of a new product proceeds on a virtual assembly line. Product managers figure out what features are likely to please customers; product designers then figure out how those features should look and feel. These designs are passed to engineering, which builds something new or modifies an existing product and, once this is done, hands it off to somebody responsible for verifying that the new product works the way the product managers and designers intended. For a product such as the iPhone, these internal handoffs may happen on a monthly or quarterly basis.

Think back one more time to the envelope-stuffing exercise. What is the most efficient way to do this work?

At IMVU, we attempted to design, develop, and ship our new features one at a time, taking advantage of the power of small batches. Here's what it looked like.

Instead of working in separate departments, engineers and designers would work together side by side on one feature at a time. Whenever that feature was ready to be tested with customers, they immediately would release a new version of the product, which would go live on our website for a relatively small number of people. The team would be able immediately to assess the impact of their work, evaluate its effect on customers, and decide what to do next. For tiny changes, the whole process might be repeated several times per day. In fact, in the aggregate, IMVU makes about fifty changes to its product (on average) every single day.

Just as with the Toyota Production System, the key to being able to operate this quickly is to check for defects immediately, thus preventing bigger problems later. For example, we had an extensive set of automated tests that assured that after every change our product still worked as designed. Let's say an engineer accidentally removed an important feature, such as the checkout button on one of our e-commerce pages. Without this button, customers no longer could buy anything from IMVU. It's as if our business instantly became a hobby. Analogously to the Toyota *andon* cord, IMVU used an elaborate set of defense mechanisms that prevented engineers from accidentally breaking something important.

We called this our product's immune system because those automatic protections went beyond checking that the product behaved as expected. We also continuously monitored the health of our business itself so that mistakes were found and removed automatically.

Going back to our business-to-hobby example of the missing checkout button, let's make the problem a little more interesting. Imagine that instead of removing the button altogether, an engineer makes a mistake and changes the button's color so that it is now white on a white background. From the point of view of automated functional tests, the button is still there and everything is working normally; from the customer's point of view, the button is gone, and so nobody can buy anything. This class of problems is hard to detect solely with automation but is still catastrophic from a business point of view. At IMVU, our immune system is programmed to detect these business consequences and automatically invoke our equivalent of the *andon* cord.

When our immune system detects a problem, a number of things happen immediately:

1. The defective change is removed immediately and automatically.
2. Everyone on the relevant team is notified of the problem.
3. The team is blocked from introducing any further changes,

preventing the problem from being compounded by future mistakes . . .

4. . . . until the root cause of the problem is found and fixed. (This root cause analysis is discussed in greater detail in Chapter 11.)

At IMVU, we called this *continuous deployment,* and even in the fast-moving world of software development it is still considered controversial.[3] As the Lean Startup movement has gained traction, it has come to be embraced by more and more startups, even those that operate mission-critical applications. Among the most cutting edge examples is Wealthfront, whose pivot was described in Chapter 8. The company practices true continuous deployment—including more than a dozen releases to customers every day—in an SEC-regulated environment.[4]

Continuous Deployment Beyond Software

When I tell this story to people who work in a slower-moving industry, they think I am describing something futuristic. But increasingly, more and more industries are seeing their design process accelerated by the same underlying forces that make this kind of rapid iteration possible in the software industry. There are three ways in which this is happening:

1. Hardware becoming software. Think about what has happened in consumer electronics. The latest phones and tablet computers are little more than a screen connected to the Internet. Almost all of their value is determined by their software. Even old-school products such as automobiles are seeing ever-larger parts of their value being generated by the software they carry inside, which controls everything from the entertainment system to tuning the engine to controlling the brakes. What can be built out of software can be modified much faster than a physical or mechanical device can.

2. Fast production changes. Because of the success of the lean manufacturing movement, many assembly lines are set up to allow each new product that comes off the line to be customized completely without sacrificing quality or cost-effectiveness. Historically, this has been used to offer the customer many choices of product, but in the future, this capability will allow the designers of products to get much faster feedback about new versions. When the design changes, there is no excess inventory of the old version to slow things down. Since machines are designed for rapid changeovers, as soon as the new design is ready, new versions can be produced quickly.

3. 3D printing and rapid prototyping tools. As just one example, most products and parts that are made out of plastic today are mass produced using a technique called injection molding. This process is extremely expensive and time-consuming to set up, but once it is up and running, it can reproduce hundreds of thousands of identical individual items at an extremely low cost. It is a classic large-batch production process. This has put entrepreneurs who want to develop a new physical product at a disadvantage, since in general only large companies can afford these large production runs for a new product. However, new technologies are allowing entrepreneurs to build small batches of products that are of the same quality as products made with injection molding, but at much lower cost and much, much faster.

The essential lesson is not that everyone should be shipping fifty times per day but that by reducing batch size, we can get through the Build-Measure-Learn feedback loop more quickly than our competitors can. The ability to learn faster from customers is the essential competitive advantage that startups must possess.

SMALL BATCHES IN ACTION

To see this process in action, let me introduce you to a company in Boise, Idaho, called SGW Designworks. SGW's specialty is rapid production techniques for physical products. Many of its clients are startups.

SGW Designworks was engaged by a client who had been asked by a military customer to build a complex field x-ray system to detect explosives and other destructive devices at border crossings and in war zones.

Conceptually, the system consisted of an advanced head unit that read x-ray film, multiple x-ray film panels, and the framework to hold the panels while the film was being exposed. The client already had the technology for the x-ray panels and the head unit, but to make the product work in rugged military settings, SGW needed to design and deliver the supporting structure that would make the technology usable in the field. The framework had to be stable to ensure a quality x-ray image, durable enough for use in a war zone, easy to deploy with minimal training, and small enough to collapse into a backpack.

This is precisely the kind of product we are accustomed to thinking takes months or years to develop, yet new techniques are shrinking that time line. SGW immediately began to generate the visual prototypes by using 3D computer-aided design (CAD) software. The 3D models served as a rapid communication tool between the client and the SGW team to make early design decisions.

The team and client settled on a design that used an advanced locking hinge to provide the collapsibility required without compromising stability. The design also integrated a suction cup/pump mechanism to allow for fast, repeatable attachment to the x-ray panels. Sounds complicated, right?

Three days later, the SGW team delivered the first physical prototypes to the client. The prototypes were machined out of aluminum directly from the 3D model, using a technique called computer numerical control (CNC) and were hand assembled by the SGW team.

The client immediately took the prototypes to its military contact for review. The general concept was accepted with a number of minor design modifications. In the next five days, another full cycle of design iteration, prototyping, and design review was completed by the client and SGW. The first production run of forty completed units was ready for delivery three and a half weeks after the initiation of the development project.

SGW realized that this was a winning model because feedback on design decisions was nearly instantaneous. The team used the same process to design and deliver eight products, serving a wide range of functions, in a twelve-month period. Half of those products are generating revenue today, and the rest are awaiting initial orders, all thanks to the power of working in small batches.

THE PROJECT TIME LINE	
Design and engineering of the initial virtual prototype	1 day
Production and assembly of initial hard prototypes	3 days
Design iteration: two additional cycles	5 days
Initial production run and assembly of initial forty units	15 days

Small Batches in Education

Not every type of product—as it exists today—allows for design change in small batches. But that is no excuse for sticking to outdated methods. A significant amount of work may be needed to enable innovators to experiment in small batches. As was pointed out in Chapter 2, for established companies looking to accelerate their innovation teams, building this platform for experimentation is the responsibility of senior management.

Imagine that you are a schoolteacher in charge of teaching math to middle school students. Although you may teach concepts in small batches, one day at a time, your overall curriculum cannot change very often. Because you must set up the curriculum in advance and teach the same concepts in the same order to every student in the classroom, you can try a new curriculum at most only once a year.

How could a math teacher experiment with small batches? Under the current large-batch system for educating students, it would be quite difficult; our current educational system was designed in the era of mass production and uses large batches extensively.

A new breed of startups is working hard to change all that. In School of One, students have daily "playlists" of their learning tasks that are attuned to each student's learning needs, based on that student's readiness and learning style. For example, Julia is way ahead of grade level in math and learns best in small groups, so her playlist might include three or four videos matched to her aptitude level, a thirty-minute one-on-one tutoring session with her teacher, and a small group activity in which she works on a math puzzle with three peers at similar aptitude levels. There are assessments built into each activity so that data can be fed back to the teacher to choose appropriate tasks for the next playlist.

This data can be aggregated across classes, schools, or even whole districts.

Now imagine trying to experiment with a curriculum by using a tool such as School of One. Each student is working at his or her own pace. Let's say you are a teacher who has a new sequence in mind for how math concepts should be taught. You can see immediately the impact of the change on those of your students who are at that point in the curriculum. If you judge it to be a good change, you could roll it out immediately for every single student; when they get to that part of the curriculum, they will get the new sequence automatically. In other words, tools like School of One enable teachers to work in much smaller batches, to the benefit of their students. (And, as tools reach wide-scale adoption, successful experiments by individual teachers can be rolled out district-, city-, or even nationwide.) This approach is having an impact and earning accolades. *Time* magazine recently included School of One in its "most innovative ideas" list; it was the only educational organization to make the list.[5]

THE LARGE-BATCH DEATH SPIRAL

Small batches pose a challenge to managers steeped in traditional notions of productivity and progress, because they believe that functional specialization is more efficient for expert workers.

Imagine you're a product designer overseeing a new product and you need to produce thirty individual design drawings. It probably seems that the most efficient way to work is in seclusion, by yourself, producing the designs one by one. Then, when you're done with all of them, you pass the drawings on to the engineering team and let them work. In other words, you work in large batches.

From the point of view of individual efficiency, working in large batches makes sense. It also has other benefits: it promotes skill building, makes it easier to hold individual contributors accountable, and, most important, allows experts to work without interruption. At least that's the theory. Unfortunately, reality seldom works out that way.

Consider our hypothetical example. After passing thirty design drawings to engineering, the designer is free to turn his or her attention to the next project. But remember the problems that came up during the envelope-stuffing exercise. What happens when engineering has questions about how the drawings are supposed to work? What if some of the drawings are unclear? What if something goes wrong when engineering attempts to use the drawings?

These problems inevitably turn into interruptions for the designer, and now those interruptions are interfering with the next large batch the designer is supposed to be working on. If the drawings need to be redone, the engineers may become idle while they wait for the rework to be completed. If the designer is not available, the engineers may have to redo the designs themselves. This is why so few products are actually built the way they are designed.

When I work with product managers and designers in companies that use large batches, I often discover that they have to redo their work five or six times for every release. One product manager I worked with was so inundated with interruptions that he took to coming into the office in the middle of the night so that he could work uninterrupted. When I suggested that he try switching the work process from large-batch to single-piece flow, he refused—because that would be inefficient! So strong is the instinct to work in large batches, that even when a large-batch system is malfunctioning, we have a tendency to blame ourselves.

Large batches tend to grow over time. Because moving the batch forward often results in additional work, rework, delays, and interruptions, everyone has an incentive to do work in ever-larger batches, trying to minimize this overhead. This is called the *large-batch death spiral* because, unlike in manufacturing, there are no physical limits on the maximum size of a batch.[6] It is possible for batch size to keep growing and growing. Eventually, one batch will become the highest-priority project, a "bet the company" new version of the product, because the company has taken such a long time since the last release. But now the managers are incentivized to increase batch size rather than ship the product. In light of how long the product has been in development, why not fix one more bug or add one more feature? Who really wants to be the manager who risked the success of this huge release by failing to address a potentially critical flaw?

I worked at a company that entered this death spiral. We had been working for months on a new version of a really cool product. The original version had been years in the making, and expectations for the next release were incredibly high. But the longer we worked, the more afraid we became of how customers would react when they finally saw the new version. As our plans became more ambitious, so too did the number of bugs, conflicts, and problems we had to deal with. Pretty soon we got into a situation in which we could not ship anything. Our launch date seemed to recede into the distance. The more work we got done, the more work we had to do. The lack of ability to ship eventually precipitated a crisis and a change of management, all because of the trap of large batches.

These misconceptions about batch size are incredibly common. Hospital pharmacies often deliver big batches of medications to patient floors once a day because it's efficient (a single trip, right?). But many of those meds get sent back to the pharmacy when a patient's orders have changed or the patient is moved or discharged, causing the pharmacy staff to do lots of rework and reprocessing (or trashing) of meds. Delivering smaller batches every four hours reduces the total workload for the pharmacy and ensures that the right meds are at the right place when needed.

Hospital lab blood collections often are done in hourly batches; phlebotomists collect blood for an hour from multiple patients and then send or take all the samples to the lab. This adds to turnaround time for test results and can harm test quality. It has become common for hospitals to bring small batches (two patients) or a single-patient flow of specimens to the lab even if they have to hire an extra phlebotomist or two to do so, because the total system cost is lower.[7]

PULL, DON'T PUSH

Let's say you are out for a drive, pondering the merits of small batches, and find yourself accidentally putting a dent in your new 2011 blue Toyota Camry. You take it into the dealership for repair and wait to hear the bad news. The repair technician tells you that you need to have the bumper replaced. He goes to check their inventory levels and tells you he has a new bumper in stock and they can complete your repair immediately. This is good news for everyone—you because you get your car back sooner and the dealership because they have a happy customer and don't run the risk of your taking the car somewhere else for repair. Also, they don't have to store your car or give you a loaner while they wait for the part to come in.

In traditional mass production, the way to avoid stockouts—not having the product the customer wants—is to keep a large inventory of spares just in case. It may be that the blue 2011

Camry bumper is quite popular, but what about last year's model or the model from five years ago? The more inventory you keep, the greater the likelihood you will have the right product in stock for every customer. But large inventories are expensive because they have to be transported, stored, and tracked. What if the 2011 bumper turns out to have a defect? All the spares in all the warehouses instantly become waste.

Lean production solves the problem of stockouts with a technique called pull. When you bring a car into the dealership for repair, one blue 2011 Camry bumper gets used. This creates a "hole" in the dealer's inventory, which automatically causes a signal to be sent to a local restocking facility called the Toyota Parts Distribution Center (PDC). The PDC sends the dealer a new bumper, which creates another hole in inventory. This sends a similar signal to a regional warehouse called the Toyota Parts Redistribution Center (PRC), where all parts suppliers ship their products. That warehouse signals the factory where the bumpers are made to produce one more bumper, which is manufactured and shipped to the PRC.

The ideal goal is to achieve small batches all the way down to single-piece flow along the entire supply chain. Each step in the line pulls the parts it needs from the previous step. This is the famous Toyota just-in-time production method.[8]

When companies switch to this kind of production, their warehouses immediately shrink, as the amount of just-in-case inventory [called work-in-progress (WIP) inventory] is reduced dramatically. This almost magical shrinkage of WIP is where lean manufacturing gets its name. It's as if the whole supply chain suddenly went on a diet.

Startups struggle to see their work-in-progress inventory. When factories have excess WIP, it literally piles up on the factory floor. Because most startup work is intangible, it's not nearly as visible. For example, all the work that goes into designing the minimum viable product is—until the moment that product is shipped—just WIP inventory. Incomplete designs, not-yet-validated assumptions, and most business plans are WIP. Almost every Lean Startup technique we've discussed so far works its magic in two ways: by converting push methods to pull and reducing batch size. Both have the net effect of reducing WIP.

In manufacturing, pull is used primarily to make sure production processes are tuned to levels of customer demand. Without this, factories can wind up making much more—or much less—of a product than customers really want. However, applying this approach to developing new products is not straightforward. Some people misunderstand the Lean Startup model as simply applying pull to customer wants. This assumes that customers could tell us what products to build and that this would act as the pull signal to product development to make them.[9]

As was mentioned earlier, this is not the way the Lean Startup model works, because customers often don't know what they want. Our goal in building products is to be able to run experiments that will help us learn how to build a sustainable business. Thus, the right way to think about the product development process in a Lean Startup is that it is responding to pull requests in the form of experiments that need to be run.

As soon as we formulate a hypothesis that we want to test, the product development team should be engineered to design and run this experiment as quickly as possible, using the smallest batch size that will get the job done. Remember that although we write the feedback loop as Build-Measure-Learn because the activities happen in that order, our planning really works in the reverse order: we figure out what we need to learn and then work backwards to see what product will work as an experiment to get that learning. Thus, it is not the customer, but rather our *hypothesis about the customer*, that pulls work from product development and other functions. Any other work is waste.

Hypothesis Pull in Clean Tech

To see this in action, let's take a look at Berkeley-based startup Alphabet Energy. Any machine or process that generates power, whether it is a motor in a factory or a coal-burning power plant, generates heat as a by-product. Alphabet Energy has developed a product that can generate electricity from this waste heat, using a new kind of material called a thermoelectric. Alphabet Energy's thermoelectric material was developed over ten years by scientists at the Lawrence Berkeley National Laboratories.

As with many clean technology products, there are huge challenges in bringing a product like this to market. While working through its leap-of-faith assumptions, Alphabet figured out early that developing a solution for waste thermoelectricity required building a heat exchanger and a generic device to transfer heat from one medium to another as well as doing project-specific engineering. For instance, if Alphabet wanted to build a solution for a utility such as Pacific Gas and Electric, the heat exchanger would have to be configured, shaped, and installed to capture the heat from a power plant's exhaust system.

What makes Alphabet Energy unique is that the company made a savvy decision early on in the research process. Instead of using relatively rare elements as materials, they decided to base their research on silicon wafers, the same physical substance that computer central processing units (CPUs) are made from. As CEO Matthew Scullin explains, "Our thermoelectric is the only one that can use low-cost semiconductor infrastructure for manufacturing." This has enabled Alphabet Energy to design and build its products in small batches.

By contrast, most successful clean technology startups have

had to make substantial early investments. The solar panel provider SunPower had to build in factories to manufacture its panels and partner with installers before becoming fully operational. Similarly, BrightSource raised $291 million to build and operate large-scale solar plants without delivering a watt to a single customer.

Instead of having to invest time and money in expensive fabrication facilities, Alphabet is able to take advantage of the massive existing infrastructure that produces silicon wafers for computer electronics. As a result, Alphabet can go from a product concept to holding a physical version in its hand in just six weeks from end to end. Alphabet's challenge has been to find the combination of performance, price, and physical shape that is a match for early customers. Although its technology has revolutionary potential, early adopters will deploy it only if they can see a clear return on investment.

It might seem that the most obvious market for Alphabet's technology would be power plants, and indeed, that was the team's initial hypothesis. Alphabet hypothesized that simple cycle gas turbines would be an ideal application; these turbines, which are similar to jet engines strapped to the ground, are used by power generators to provide energy for peak demand. Alphabet believed that attaching its semiconductors to those turbines would be simple and cheap.

The company went about testing this hypothesis in small batches by building small-scale solutions for its customers as a way of learning. As with many initial ideas, their hypothesis was disproved quickly. Power companies have a low tolerance for risk, making them unlikely to become early adopters. Because it wasn't weighed down by a large-batch approach, Alphabet was ready to pivot after just three months of investigation.

Alphabet has eliminated many other potential markets as well, leading to a series of customer segment pivots. The company's current efforts are focused on manufacturing firms, which have the ability to experiment with new technologies in separate parts of their factory; this allows early adopters to evaluate the real-world benefits before committing to a larger deployment. These early deployments are putting more of Alphabet's assumptions to the test. Unlike in the computer hardware business, customers are not willing to pay top dollar for maximum performance. This has required significant changes in Alphabet's product, configuring it to achieve the lowest cost per watt possible.

All this experimentation has cost the company a tiny fraction of what other energy startups have consumed. To date, Alphabet has raised approximately $1 million. Only time will tell if they will prevail, but thanks to the power of small batches, they will be able to discover the truth much faster.[10]

o o o

The Toyota Production System is probably the most advanced system of management in the world, but even more impressive is the fact that Toyota has built the most advanced learning organization in history. It has demonstrated an ability to unleash the creativity of its employees, achieve consistent growth, and produce innovative new products relentlessly over the course of nearly a century.[11]

This is the kind of long-term success to which entrepreneurs should aspire. Although lean production techniques are powerful, they are only a manifestation of a high-functioning organization that is committed to achieving maximum performance by employing the right measures of progress over the long term. Process is only the foundation upon which a great company culture can develop. But without this foundation, efforts to encourage learning, creativity, and innovation will fall flat—as many disillusioned directors of HR can attest.

The Lean Startup works only if we are able to build an organization as adaptable and fast as the challenges it faces. This requires tackling the human challenges inherent in this new way of working; that is the subject of the remainder of Part Three.

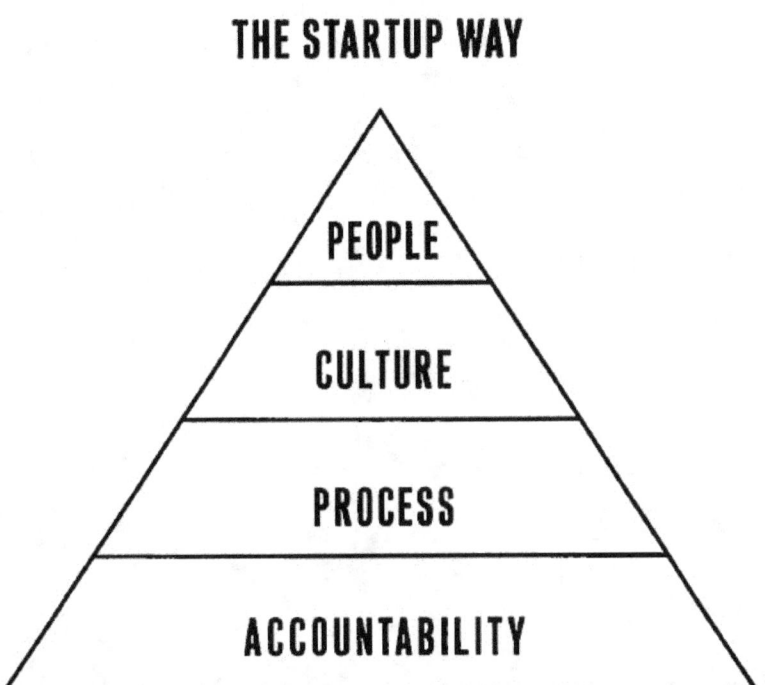

www.ingramcontent.com/pod-product-compliance
Lightning Source LLC
Chambersburg PA
CBHW080931220526
45465CB00008BA/3011